A Soul In Place
Reclaiming Home As Sacred Space

by Carol Bridges

Publisher's Cataloging in Publication
(Prepared by Quality Books Inc.)

Bridges, Carol Margaret, 1942-
  A soul in place : reclaiming home as sacred space / by Carol Bridges.
    p. cm.
    Includes index.
    ISBN 0-945111-11-8

  1. Feng-shui. 2. Interior decoration.   I. Title.

BF1779.F4.B75 1995   133.3'33
                                      QBI95-20308

Earth Nation Publishing
P.O. Box 743
Nashville, IN 47448

Illustrations: collage by Carol Bridges, computer enhancements by Dwight Sands

Manufactured in the United States of America
10 9 8 7 6 5 4 3 2 1

ISBN 0-945111-11-8, perfectbound edition, $15.00

Dedication

I dedicate this book to my mother, Margaret Wall, and to my grandmothers, Margaret Chandler and Margaret Wall, who provided all of the nourishing places of my childhood.

Acknowledgements

Special thanks to Christopher Alexander whose writings on place spoke so clearly to my soul and to Master Lin Yun and Sarah Rossbach who brought the art of feng shui to my time and place. I also acknowledge Kevin Eggers for providing my first amazing experience of how space can be arranged to dramatically alter one's consciousness. I am deeply thankful to Dwight Sands for his computer art wizardry and everlasting encouragement. Thanks to Wendy Allen, Bonnie Hunt, Diane DeWall and Barbara Stahura for the valuable manuscript feedback. Thanks to all the places where the "walk to town" is still possible and pleasurable and to all of the people who preserve those places.

Table of Contents

Other Books by Carol Bridges

The Medicine Woman Inner Guidebook, A Woman's Guide To Her Unique Powers

The Medicine Woman Tarot

Secrets Stored In Ecstasy

The Medicine Woman's Guide To Being In Business For Yourself, How To Live By Your Spiritual Vision In A Money-Based World

How To Use This Book

The ideas in this book are based, in part, upon an ancient Chinese system of environmental harmonies called feng shui (pronounced "fung shway"). Feng shui means "wind and water." Like wind and water which move constantly through all life forms, the principles of feng shui underlie all of the ideas I have put forth. Yet, this is not a feng shui text. Instead, this book is a compilation of material which, when I experienced it, made my soul feel at home. This is material which gave all of my longings a place, a reason to be and a space to dwell. This is material which affirms our innate wisdom about spaces and their effects upon us. Some of it comes from dance, from meditation, and from study of the body's and the psyche's response to form as it appears everywhere around us. It comes also from scholarly study of the works of many building and landscape architects, ecologists, artists and poets as well as native people and world spiritual traditions which recognize the environment as also "God," a divine creation which can lift us to the highest experiences.

According to feng shui, there are nine life endeavors around which our lives revolve. These are 1) career, 2) self-knowledge, 3) ancestors, 4) wealth, 5) fame, 6) marriage, 7) children, 8) helpful people, and 9) health. We will explore each endeavor as it takes place in our home, our society and our self. The buildings in which we spend most of our waking hours can enhance our enjoyment and success in each endeavor

1

or limit and, at times, completely undermine our best intentions and dreams. Each chapter explores a way of arranging our environment so that our potential for success is maximized and our soul is, at the same time, recognized and nourished.

For the purpose of assisting you with the design of your home environment, I have divided each life endeavor into seven features. There could be many more features listed. You may wish to add some of your own. The features are ways you can arrange your built, purchased or collected objects and living plants, stones, fire and water to create pathways and passages for blessed life-giving energy to travel through your home, workplace and community. The features are designed to enhance the enjoyment or encourage the success of each life endeavor. The more features you are able to arrange for yourself, the greater will be your personal sense of place and fulfillment, though even one small shift in your surroundings can often eliminate stress and bring relief from feeling trapped, lost, scattered or depressed.

You can read the book from front to back and it will take you from the approach to your home through nine life endeavors that take place in the spaces you occupy, then outside your home's boundaries again to the community at large. Or, you can just read the section on a particular life endeavor that needs enhancing and read through the seven features to glean suggestions on ways to environmentally correct the imbalance. The features which enhance each endeavor will provide the key elements that you can use in adjusting your environment to bring about success in that life situation.

Each feature is both a quality and an element of place. The features are ordinary everyday things put together in such a way that your soul feels nourished and energized by the arrangement. Our experience of life is mostly a feeling thing. In every endeavor, the actual physical achievement of our goal has little value to us unless the process of achieving it and continuing to relate to it feels good.

Play with the ideas offered herein. Feng shui rhymes with fun and play. It is a joyful refreshment of your surroundings, and yet, it can be taken as deep as your spirit will allow. After each chapter, there are three attunements listed: a presenting issue, a movement, and an affirmation. The presenting issue is a sentence or two you might hear yourself or your client saying. This will key you in to the feature that might need attention in her or his environment. The movement is a suggested body exercise that will help you or your client feel in your body the physical and spiritual effects that the feature is trying to actualize in your environment of place. The affirmation seeds your mind with the thought that will help you or your client out of the predicament indicated by the presenting issue. The movement and affirmation begin to create inner sacred space while you attend to the process of creating outer sacred space.

All of the attunements are to help you to listen to your soul when you read and when you make the suggested changes in your home, furnishings and gardens. Try things out. Sit with them for a day or two. Let yourself feel and be moved. Because we are all unique, you will probably find yourself doing something a little differently than any of the suggestions I make. This is as it should be. I hope this book to be food for the soul, garnished by the special flavors of your individual life. Savor each lesson until coming home is the feast it should always be.

The Nine Life Endeavors

The purpose of this book is to awaken you to the energetic relationship between you, your furnishings, your home, your feelings, your opinions about life, the life rewards you reap and the fate of the Earth. Everything great and small is connected. Every little thought and thing which makes up our daily world of details in some way shifts and moves the entire fabric of creation. Likewise, we ourselves are moved through moods and cycles by all that exists around us.

There are large forces of nature and of society over which we seem to have little or no control. Yet, feng shui teaches - and I have profoundly experienced - that we can take command of our personal domain, however small, and in so doing shift the course of fate.

Feng shui is very specific in offering simple adjustments we can make in our homes when we want to change our luck in a particular area. For in depth study, I highly recommend that you read Sarah Rossbach's books listed in the Recommended Reading at the back of this book, take one of my workshops and attend a lecture by Master Lin Yun.

A Soul In Place is meant only to awaken you to the spiritual importance of how you arrange your "place in the world," the home you dwell within. We will, therefore, explore the nine life endeavors as starting points, places to open your eyes and see new connections between such things as doors and life's passages, colors and the vitality of your existence, chairs and your stature in the society. Everything around you is speaking metaphorically. All you have to do is look and listen. This will feed your intuition. Your intuition will guide you to a deep understanding of the relationship of all life.

Career - Your home and its presentation to strangers, its streetside appearance, says volumes to anyone passing by. That first impression may be the only chance you get to make the impact you desire. Secondarily, your home affects your career by offering the needed respite from your job so that you can pursue your career fresh each day. A soul needs not only a geographical spot to dwell in body, but a place in society where its talents and skills are valued. Finding this place is not just a matter of job-hunting, but also of creating the work area, gathering the tools, and providing the furnishings which support the work your soul came to do.

Self-Knowledge - Another function of home is to give yourself a place to explore the deeper you, to expand your knowledge in your areas of interest. A soul is born to grow. It needs a place to learn, to solve problems, to synthesize information and to be still, touching again upon its divine origin.

Ancestors - A soul also wants to be reminded of its connection to infinite time. It wants to know the richness of life experience out of which it came to be born. It wants a place in history. You give it this by honoring your lineage and/or the native people of the land you live upon.

Wealth - A soul pursues wealth, reaching to find the true meaning and experience of the word. The soul gathers to itself symbols of what it deems to be "the good life" to remind it of its heavenly home and its mission to restore the natural wealth of the planet. Your home clearly depicts your view of wealth, propriety and ecology. Your soul displays its values.

Fame - It is not necessary to be a legend or a star, but every soul needs recognition. Every person has a reputation. Your soul wants yours to be a good one. When your name is brought to mind, words, images and feelings are associated with you. What people think of you is important to your soul. When others look at your home, they store this knowledge as a portion of your standing in their community. You have a place on the ladder of success in their minds.

Marriage - A soul may not need a wedding and a certificate, but it usually needs a "significant other" to be a soul-sharing partner. The soul seeks one person that it deems to be of like mind. Your home must be inviting to such a soul, for he/she will be dwelling there too.

Children - Not everyone has them, but everyone is one at some time. Think of children as the creative part of yourself. A soul is all about creation. That is the life game it plays on a grand scale, but it also likes the opportunity to create when the stakes are small, where errors do not matter much, just for the fun of it. Your home is the place for your soul to play.

Helpful People - We wish a great benefactor would come to our door, offer us a check for a million dollars, in other words, a ticket to our dream-come-true. A soul needs support in this world of challenges. It, therefore, must maximize its chances of receiving help by inviting people to its home or travelling to other places to meet them. A soul needs a place to find them.

Health - The soul suffers or its human life ends if there is not health in the body. The Earth has blessed all souls by providing abundant nourishment everywhere. Unfortunately, some human beings became greedy and short-sighted in their treatment of this bounty and now we all suffer many ills because of it. We must restore health in our planet, in ourselves. Our souls long for "the Garden," the place where we have only to reach out and grab a fresh peach or dip into the clear stream for a drink. Our souls have some work to do here. Start at home, in the center of your life. Let your heart create the hearth that nourishes your soul and restores the life of our home planet Earth.

The nine life endeavors are the pursuits which take place all our lives. We must give them each a place which maximizes our chances of success.

The Presenting Issues

The following is a list of statements you might hear yourself or your client make, complaints about life that can be changed by "rearranging the furniture." This list allows you to quickly go to the chapter which relates to the area of life under duress. Though no claims can be made that moving chairs, tables and beds will cure every illness or life crisis, the shift in outlook can be the beginning of the healing process.

Our intent must be to honor the life circumstances which are occuring and to rearrange the environment in such a way as to restore balance and harmony as best we can. Often, just realizing that your environment can offer some nourishment in a time of need relaxes stress and gives the soul the breath of free time it needs to bring about an intellectual, emotional or spiritual solution. The creation of this "sacred space" is what we are after.

Chaos
"My home does not feel good. I experience chaos at home and want to leave. I find that I am going out often without good reason." See **Sacred Space.**

Fluctuating Luck
"My luck is fluctuating dramatically for no apparant reason." See **Wild Grace.**

Invaded
"Life is too hard. I feel up against the wall. I am always having to overcome obstacles. I often feel invaded." See Career Feature #1, **Natural Barrier.**

A Soul in Place

Left Out
"I feel like I am being left out or overlooked. I cannot seem to get what I want." See Career Feature #2, **Entrancing Gateway**.

Pressured
"I feel like things happen too fast. Sometimes I feel hemmed in, up tight or like too much is required of me." See Career Feature #3, **Gently Winding Path**.

Inadequate
"I feel as though I never quite reach my destination. I do not achieve my goals. I never get anywhere." See Career Feature #4, **Feeling of Arrival**.

Bothered
"No one respects me. I am always interrupted." See Career Feature #5, **Aura of Authority**.

Dull
"I am bored. My guests struggle to get acquainted. I do not know how to "break the ice" when entertaining." See Career Feature #6, **Fascinating Spot**.

Blocked
"I feel blocked, squeezed and misdirected." See Career Feature #7, **Easy Passage**.

Confused
"I have no place to retreat. I am tired, confused or sick. I do not know who I am or what I want." See Self-Knowledge Feature #1, **Private Oasis**.

Overwhelmed
"I feel overwhelmed, restricted or hemmed in." See Self-Knowledge Feature #2, **Walls Which Protect**.

Dead
"I feel cold. I experience some sense of deadness in my being. There are dead trees or plants around the house." See Self-Knowledge Feature #3, **Plants, Growth and Flowering**.

Meaningless
"I feel disconnected from life. Nothing has any meaning." See Self-Knowledge Feature #4, **Personally Meaningful Ornament**.

Restless

"I have no dreams. I feel restless." See Self-Knowledge Feature #5, **Dream-stirring Comfort.**

Disconnected
"I feel disconnected from the Source." See Self-Knowledge Feature #6, **Devotional Offering.**

Depressed
"I feel ill, depressed. My energy is low." See Self-Knowledge Feature #7, **Raising the Chi.**

Lost
"I have no one to guide me. I did not receive the training I needed for life. I feel shortchanged." See Ancestors Feature #1, **Soil, Stone and Body.**

Alone
"I have lost my family through separation, divorce or death." See Ancestors Feature #2, **Gathering of Kin.**

Unacceptable
"I feel odd. I feel unaccepted." See Ancestors Feature #3, **My Place Among Others.**

Unlucky
"My luck has changed since I moved here. The house feels cold, dark or negative. Prior owners had bad times." See Ancestors Feature #4, **History of Happenings.**

Rootless
"I feel rootless. I do not understand why others behave the way they do." See Ancestors Feature #5, **Tradition Honored.**

Handicapped
"I feel handicapped, disadvantaged or insecure." See Ancestors Feature #6, **Tools That Work.**

Angry
"I am angry. I am bothered when things wear out or break. I do not want to grow old myself." See Ancestors Feature #7, **Death and Decay.**

Overpowered
"I have no control over the situation. Others overpower me." See Wealth

A Soul in Place

Feature #1, **Place of Command.**

Purposeless
"I am not sure what I am working for. I do not know my purpose in life." See Wealth Feature #2, **Holdings In Sight.**

Dissatisfied
"I feel overwhelmed by outer circumstances. I tend to go on shopping sprees, but I am seldom satisfied with my purchases."
See Wealth Feature #3, **Paper, Trees and Books.**

Messy
"My life is a mess. I find myself wanting to be bossy and control others." See Wealth Feature #4, **Establishment of Order.**

Afraid of foreigners
"I am afraid of others. I judge others harshly." See Wealth Feature #5, **Information Station.**

Insecure
"I feel insecure. There is not enough. I am always working but never quite seeing what I get for it." See Wealth Feature # 6, **Water, Flow and Vision.**

Vulnerable
"I am afraid of theft and disaster." See Wealth Feature #7, **Safe Shelter.**

Unknown
"No one knows who I really am." See Fame Feature #1, **Reputation.**

Timid
"I am uncertain of others' opinions of me. I do not trust peole." See Fame Feature #2, **Observation Places.**

Unheard
"Others do not listen to me. I am afraid to speak up." See Fame Feature #3, **Wind, Sound and Voice.**

Rejected
"I am not having fun. I am not supported by others. I feel unloved and unhappy." See Fame Feature #4, **Clan of Encouragement.**

Tense

"I feel tense, tight, constricted." See Fame Feature #5, **Giveaway**.

Disappointed
"I never seem to achieve my goals. My successes are shortlived." See Fame Feature #6, **Obstacles Overcome**.

Overworked
"There is not enough time." See Fame Feature #7, **Pause, Receive Blessings**.

Longing
"There is no romance in my life. There is not enough show of affection." See Marriage Feature #1, **Place To Embrace**.

Melancholy
"I feel lackadaisical, worn out, overly sentimental." See Marriage Feature #2, **Light, Warmth and Desire**.

At loose ends
"I feel lost. I have no sense of home." See Marriage Feature #3, **Surprise of Sweet Smells**.

Distant
"No one talks to me. I experience a lack of intimacy with others." See Marriage Feature #4, **Intimate Nook**.

Lonely
"We have no privacy as a couple. There is a lack of closeness in our relationship. I have no close relationship." See Marriage Feature #5, **Inspiration For Two**.

Confined
"I feel confined, dull and bored." See Marriage Feature #6, **Variety of Texture**.

Joyless
"I feel overworked. I lack joy in my life." See Marriage Feature #7, **Luxurious Lounging**.

Uptight
"I am afraid to make mistakes." See Children Feature #1, **Creative Play**.

Restricted
"I feel restricted and confined." See Children Feature #2, **Room To Roam**.

A Soul in Place

Old
"I am afraid of growing old." See Children Feature #3, **Shifts and Transitions**.

Foolish
"I feel unappreciated and stifled. I am afraid to look foolish." See Children Feature #4, **Interests Indulged**.

Friendless
"I find it hard to make friends." See Children Feature #5, **Cozy Place To Listen**.

Nostalgic
"There is no more magic in my life. I long for days gone by." See Children Feature #6, **Secret Treasures**.

Gloomy
"I feel in the dark about things. I seem to attract shady characters into my life." See Children Feature #7, **Illumination**.

Urge to wander
"I am discontent. I blame myself for not being happy, feeling I should be thankful for what I have." See Helpful People Feature #1, **Readiness Meets Opportunity**.

Shy
"I am shy. I find it hard to meet others." See Helpful People Feature #2, **Cruising and Courting**.

Isolated
"It seems as though I spend half my life in a car. I am out of touch with friends, family, neighbors and nature." See Helpful People Feature #3, **Easy Stroll**.

Ugly
"Life is ugly. I feel ugly." See Helpful People Feature #4, **View From the Mountain**.

Out of sorts
"I feel out of sorts. I sense something is wrong, but I do not know what." See Helpful People Feature #5, **Traveller's Eye**.

Irritated
"I often complain about others. My disposition is bad." See Helpful People

14

Feature #6, **Correction of Misuse.**

Ungrounded
"I am lonely. I feel isolated. I do not feel at home here." See Helpful People
Feature #7, **Beneficial Relationship.**

Over the hill
"The places I loved are gone. I feel I cannot return to an earlier, better time."
See Health Feature #1, **Hint of a Spirit.**

Stuck
"I do not want to go out. I feel like hibernating." See Health Feature #2,
Invitation To Enter.

Unimportant
"I feel unimportant." See Health Feature #3, **Seed of Self.**

Sick
"I lack a sense of well-being." See Health Feature #4, **Hidden Sanctuary.**

Victimized
"I often feel the world is against me." See Health Feature #5, **Nature's
Intention.**

Homeless
"I am upset with others who seem to be able to care for themselves. I am
burdened with the complexity of life." See Health Feature #6, **A Place To Be
Poor.**

Hopeless
"I fear death. I cannot let go. I lack trust in Creation." See Health Feature #7,
Rest At the End.

Space and Grace

20th Century zen koan:
"How does one know when the furniture is arranged just right?"

The Two Basics

1. Space, the area in which life takes place.
2. Grace, the energy which animates life.

Sacred Space

We are once again returning to our homes as priestesses and priests, guardians of the temple. We may be corporate executives, massage therapists, or clerks in a store, but whatever our outer career, we are also the makers of home. Somewhere deep inside we have longed for the right to return to our temples, to once again have the space we care for be revered. Our souls want to go home.

Home is not merely a building. It is a feeling. It is a sense of knowing and being known. It is a place of safety, of self-expression, of play, of making love, and of loving the life we see around us. We have been temple keepers since time began, symbolizing our relationship to the cosmos by the shape and design of our buildings. Sacred space and home were one for most traditional peoples. A Tsuri (Native Americans of Northern California) legend says, "A person's first commitment must be to home."

To all native people, home was Nature and the gifts of wood, stone and grasses she offered which women and men then arranged into a shelter. That dwelling was a spiritual link to the great forces of life. Homes were often circular in design to honor the circle of life, the cycle of seasons. Whatever the shape, it had a symbolic meaning. Places of worship were designed to reach to what the people believed to be the Source of Life, either dug deep into the Earth or with spires high in the sky. The energies of the sacred spaces were kept pure by a constant honoring of the Creative Source. Craftsmanship was perfected in order to honor the Sacred Beings who dwelled in the Source, for beauty has always been considered an attribute of God.

We live now in a time when much that was considered the Sacred Mystery has been explained away "scientifically." If something cannot be measured, it is thought not to exist. Magic is taboo. Imagination is delegated to children and performing artists. And worship is confined to church on Sunday. But this viewpoint is falling away. Temples are emerging from the mists. Sacred places are showing their faces. And the voice of the Priestess or Priest within is saying, build the altar again.

No matter what your religious persuasion, you probably remember or were told of a time in the past when altars were a part of every home, when guests were honored as gods, and saints and angels or leprechauns and fairies were expected to drop by. The woman of the house kept the prayers and petitions, arranged the healings and celebrations, presided at birth and at death, all with the respect she deserved for keeping the peace and showing the way to the Light.

Powerful forces have tried to undermine women's relationship to Spirit and Nature, but the burnings did not stop us, nor will the nuclear age. Society suffers if home is not kept. Violence erupts. Illness breaks out. Addiction and abuse become rampant. People at every level feel isolated and homeless. Seeing this, we rise again, to take up the tending of the hearth. Secretaries and steamfitters, stewardesses and stateswomen are making sacred the temple of home. We realize, whether it is a man or a woman doing the job, a part-time or a full-time vocation, someone must tend the hearth fires. Without caretaking this sacred place, the heart of our life stops beating.

This is not a plea to put women back into powerless positions, but to raise up the place of home in the eyes of men, women and children. For when home is treated as sacred space, all activities there and out in the world take a turn for the better. Any system of giving life meaning when applied to the home deepens your experience of the sacred in all things. To dwell in a spiritualized house is to live in the Mystery of Love.

You may already have a secret spot that is the altar of your awakening. I have seen candles and icons in the back of closets, carefully tied bundles of special collected stones, photographs of family arranged in an intuitively magical array. The seed is there. But what if you could also arrange your whole house according to cosmic principles that actually brought harmony to every aspect of your life? There are such systems. The most fascinating one I have encountered is called "feng shui." It is an ancient Chinese art of placement whereby everything from your tabletop to your town can be laid out in specific harmonies with the forces of nature. In my work, I draw heavily from this tradition, yet integrate it with studies done on timeless architecture and patterns of living which have been shown to have a worldwide appeal.

I have attempted to bring the essence of these bodies of knowledge to this book and the Wild Grace system of reclaiming sacred space explained in the next chapter. Let us define for our purposes here, the meaning of sacred space. It is not "sacred sites," as in the famous geographical places such as Stonehenge and Macchu Picchu. These are particular strong vortices of earth energy, recognized, honored and used by previous earth inhabitants. We will look at our homes as more subtle energy fields, but we will treat them in somewhat the same way as a sacred site should be treated.

We will give the sun a special welcome, treat the stones to respectful placement, perhaps arrange for sighting of the stars and moon, and give the water a chance to sing. We will arrange furniture, plants, and trees so that their placement acts as a conductor of emotions and, therefore, life. We will use the tiniest things to pick up spirits, like laughter, happiness, and awe. We will make places for cleansing and mending the heart, not just cleaning and sleep. We will find the nourishing place and the spot of fascination, the shapes and views which protect us or expand our horizons. We will give home its sacred task, the restoration of our souls. And thus, again, we will know ourselves as priest or priestess of the realm. Let the whole-ing and souling of our homes begin.

Presenting Issue: My home does not feel good. I experience chaos at home and want to leave. I find that I am going out often without good reason.

Movement: Stand with feet shoulder width apart, knees relaxed, pelvis balanced over your feet. Reach to the sky. Bring your hands down, palms together, fingers pointing up, in front of your heart, as in the prayer position. Imagine yourself in sacred space.

Affirmation: My home is my temple. The Spirit dwells within.

Wild Grace

Imagine, if you will, some wondrous blessing from the heavens. A grace. Yet this blessing cannot be stereotyped and easily contained. Sometimes it offers surprises beyond our highest hopes. Sometimes it arrives when we least expect it. Sometimes, it waits for just the right moment or acts in strange but inspiring ways that stimulate you to take action now. Imagine too, that this grace is a spirit with a changing form.

She has been Lady Luck, Sleeping Beauty, the Muse and the Divine Child.

For the grace is wild. It has not yet been tamed and made to bow to the forms of a particular religion, nor place and time. It comes when the conditions welcome it, or shall we say, her. For if you can see the grace as a woman for now, it will hclp us to work together and to energize your home in a way that will allow the grace to visit in all of her forms with all of her blessings and surprises.

I first met Wild Grace when I was struggling to fix up an old house, one that was built before building codes, by a person who must have had short legs when he entered the front door and long ones when he went out the back! The steps in front had five inch risers and the ones down from the back porch had ten. The rest of the house followed this pattern in subtle and irritating ways.

But the land upon which the house sat was beautiful. So I endured the idiosyncracies of the building and played with the garden. The more I dug and shoveled, moved rocks and planted flowers, the more the trees and waters took on a special feeling. It was as if the wind spoke to me and the wooden beams whispered. They said, "Don't give up. Do what you can." So I did.

I worked with the walls and I painted the floors and I shored up the sags and made dark into light. I tore out a wall and made the curtains just right. It became a poetic journey to the Spirit of Light. I moved my desk to the window. I looked out with glee. It was Wild Grace that was coming to bestow blessings upon me! How did she appear? Not as a woman in physical form you could see, but a sense from the tall trees and the wildflowers out back, that my home in the hills was no longer a shack.

Please excuse the simple rhyme, but I want to impart the sense of lightness that overcame me as I began to put the principles to work that I introduce here for you. Indeed, an introduction is all that I can make, because a relationship must be formed between you and the spirit of your place. Then from the bond that forms between you, will come instructions beyond this book. Your land, your home will have a voice, and perhaps her name will come. She will tell you one day, in her own way.

Now, begin to get a sense of your house and land as a being. There may be parts of this being that are neglected, parts that are respected. Assess the situation. You may be building anew, starting from scratch, or working, like I was, with just what you have. The best thing about creating sacred space is that it costs next to nothing. And it is all the more healing to the planet if you are fixing-up and recycling than if you are out purchasing new.

A small apartment on a city street or a huge estate are equally suitable as sacred space. For, as you will see, it is an attitude of reverence coupled with an awareness of nature's way and knowledge of a system, like feng shui, which relates the cosmos to the mundane that sets the stage for deeply meaningful experience in your home and in your world.

Presenting Issue: My luck is fluctuating dramatically for no apparant reason.

Movement: Standing with feet shoulder width apart, body relaxed, imagine an energy from the center of the Earth coming up through the soles of your feet and travelling throughout your body. Feel it starting to fill your toes, your feet, your ankles, your lower legs, etc., one body part at a time.

Affirmation: I welcome my guest Wild Grace. She transforms both my inner and my outer space.

Career

You have found your career when what your hands are doing agrees with what your heart is feeling.

The Seven Features of the Career Endeavor

1. Natural Barrier
2. Entrancing Gateway
3. Gently Winding Path
4. Feeling of Arrival
5. Aura of Authority
6. Fascinating Spot
7. Easy Passage

Natural Barrier
Feature #1 of the Career Endeavor

We will begin our study with a view of your home from the street, a perspective just outside your place, looking at your property with a stranger's eye. Here is where you make the daily transition from the world "out there" to your own personal private domain. How easy is it to enter your private world? Can anyone walk right in? Or is there something visible or invisible stopping them? What resistance do you meet from within as you approach your home?

There are two kinds of natural barriers, one is designed by nature's landscape - the line of a river, the grove of trees, the edge of a cliff. The other is the mindset which keeps you from seeing things anew when you have become used to thinking about them in a certain way. This book is to help you overcome this mental barrier and see your land, home and workplace* with fresh eyes.

As every life endeavor TAKES PLACE, place is of the utmost importance in how we feel during the endeavor. A bank president whose home is a small city apartment surrounded by traffic noise and hordes of people will experience the job differently than one who lives in a pleasant Vermont neighborhood in a vintage stone house with antique furnishings and views of the hills, even though their careers are the same.

Your career may take place primarily outside of home, but your home can still assist or detract from your career. Your home is always telling you how you are doing. In particular, the feeling upon arrival gives everyone, including yourself, an impression about your success. Whether you entertain clients or your primary visitor is your mother, the experience each has upon entering your home will affect your relationship with them.

Life is lived in place. Place affects our feelings and our actions. In any place, we are in relationship to the earth, the air, the sunlight, and the water. We can arrange our places to draw upon these forces in ways which give us feelings of well-being. Feeling safe, serene, comfortable, and intermittently excited, we are likely to be happy and successful. Our life endeavors will feel good to the soul.

Think about the space you are occupying now. What are the natural environmental barriers between you and the forces over which you have little control such as rivers, busy streets, rainstorms, intruders, airplane noise and neighboring buildings. Check the area for potential irritating or damaging forces such as heavy traffic noise or possible floods, and see if nature has already given you a barrier to moderate or keep these forces out. You will want some kind of barrier between yourself and any disruptive forces. You are fortunate if nature has already protected your land with trees, hills or other pleasant natural barriers.

After you have become aware of the nearby forces over which you have little control and acknowledged nature's protective gifts, you can then begin to build what is still needed. Never approach land with the idea of clearing it before you check into the purpose of natural barriers already in place. If you can, use biological controls such as trees or any other plants, rocks or bermed soil to subdue noise and moderate heat, a pond or fountain for cooling, or a hedge for privacy, as these are long-lasting and add beauty and life chi. ("Chi" - pronounced "chee" - is the Chinese word for life force energy.) Then bring in fences and walls, if needed, which compliment the whole.

How much protection do you need? A tall fence too close is imprisoning. A dark wall in front of a window's view is foreboding. Wall out only ugliness, excessive noise, intruders and potential disasters. Open up to beauty, light, panoramic vistas and pleasant visitors. If you do not have a good view, paint one!

Pay attention to the balance of sunlight and shadow coming into your yard and house, as these affect your daily mood. Outdoors, people generally seek sunlight to warm themselves and like looking into dappled shade for its interesting ever-changing patterns. Inside, sun is used to energize during the waking hours. Is there a place where it can shine upon your daily work? Sun, of course, provides needed radiant heat on cool days and will give you more than heat bill savings in the dark winter season. People who do not receive enough sunlight suffer from a disease called S.A.D., seasonal affective disorder, which is a depressed and melancholy feeling.

Look at your home, your land and your workplace now in terms of what is fenced in and what is fenced out. Where are you protected and where are you vulnerable? Do you feel comfortable with this balance? Walk around outside. What simple rearrangements could be made to offer more protection from negative influences or to bring in more light according to your prcfcrcncc?

The barriers you choose should feel like borders, not obstacles to overcome. A border defines what is yours, that place where your heart and hands have agreed to work together for the good of your soul.

Presenting Issue: Life is too hard. I feel up against the wall. I am always having to overcome obstacles. I often feel invaded.

Movement: Beginning at the top of your head, feel your skin. Bring your hands down your face, arms, trunk and legs. After feeling your fleshy body boundary, extend your arms in front of you, palms facing your heart. Bring your hands very slowly toward your body, feeling the subtle resistance in your energy field where your hands tend to pause. Simply become aware of this.

You will notice in the course of interaction with other people, that you have an energy field layer of yourself that you prefer strangers do not penetrate. Find your comfortable energy boundaries.

Affirmation: My boundaries are clear. Thus protected, only friendly forces enter my space.

Entrancing Gateway
Feature #2 of the Career Endeavor

Somewhere in the natural or human-made barrier between your home and the outside world, there must be an opening. Here you invite others to enter. Here you en-trance them. The qualities most relevant to any entrance are: invitation, welcome, and revelation. Who do you want to invite into your space? If you are considering the gateway to your home, and your house is in a very busy downtown neighborhood close to the street with many strangers passing by, you may want a gateway that says, "keep out unless invited." An ornamental iron locking gate or a tall hedge bordering a narrow entry passage might serve this purpose.

On the other hand, if your home is down at the end of a country lane, you might be inclined to welcome all visitors by leaving the yard wide open to the house, the gateway defined only by a winding path lined with flowers. A home where many business associates will be dropping in may need a more formal entrance which speaks of impeccable care and clear contracts between you and your land.

You reveal in your entryway, to your customers or friends, just what it is you want them to know about you at first meeting. Your gateway is a first impression place. It can entrance the visitor by its intriguing objects. Perhaps you collect antiques; your fence could be an antique itself. An accountant might want a very tidy lawn, showing attention to detail. A health care professional might make a statement with a gateway and yard that is lean, strong and clean in design. If you love to play, your gateway may be done with a fantasy touch.

Look at the place of entry to your home. Who is it you are inviting? Are they the kinds of people you enjoy? What kind of objects would make them feel instantly at home as they approach your place? In what small way could you reveal to them who you are and what you do? The gateway is not the place to "let it all show," but to intrigue the visitor and make her or him feel that you just might be worth knowing or that your place shows a promise or possibility of something very good happening inside.

To get ideas, go for a drive. What kind of person lives in the house with a lawn full of yard art? Might they be fun to know? Do you expect lawyers live there? Mom and Pop? Who do you imagine lives in the dark brick house with the curtains always closed and the overgrown bushes reaching out into the path? Someone with something to hide? You will see that your imagination is easily carried into fantasies of the kinds of people who live in the various homes you pass. Often, you will find yourself forming opinions about their careers and whether or not you would like to interact with the residents as people.

Now drive by your home.

Presenting Issue: I feel like I am being left out or overlooked. I cannot seem to get what I want.

Movement: Experiment with movements that invite. By your gestures, invite pleasure, then business, then trouble. How is each invitation written in a glance, a frown, a gesture?

Affirmation: I attract all who interest me into relationship to myself. I welcome, in them, the Divinity.

Gently Winding Path
Feature #3 of the Career Endeavor

The human being, like all organic things, is made of curves and feels at home among them. Although there are places where you might want to bring about a more controlled and limiting feeling with straight walks, generally, even short paths are best with a curve.

On the winding path, the person is asked to proceed slowly, the path guiding her or him first to look in one direction, then another. This brings about a sense of familiarity with all surroundings and thus a feeling of safety as well. A slow walk allows a person to pay attention to the walk itself, to take in scenic views and interesting details.

The texture and width of the path must be in keeping with the atmosphere you are trying to create in your total landscape. The narrower path is more intimate. It its widest part is "streetside" and it narrows as you get to the house or garden destination, it will funnel people to the focal point and also allow those leaving to have a sense of expanding back into the larger world.

If the path is richly textured, such as with stones or creeping plants, the experience of walking upon it will be more sensual than if the path is so smooth that you do not notice it beneath your feet. Assuming you wish to captivate the attention of whoever walks upon the path, you will want to vary the texture of the path, yet repeat your materials to form a pattern. This can be done with stones with creeping plants between them or bricks or boards with grass and flowers alongside, or any number of ways. There are many excellent books published on specific path-building materials and plants to enhance your walkway. Refer to these when you are ready to choose the embellishments of your basic design. An inviting path says, "Welcome, I am a person who cares to make your journey interesting."

Occasionally, you will see a house where there is no path at all to the front door because it is not used or where two paths are seen at once by a guest, each leading to a different door.   This throws your visitors off balance by causing uncertainty. The unused door is an example of intent at cross purposes. The house designer's intent to place the door where it is, is at odds with your current intent not to use that door as an entrance. This "mixed message" cannot be deciphered by Wild Grace, and she will not leave her blessings at your door. In other words, chi does not flow clearly through intent in opposition.

A feng shui practitioner can perform a ceremony which can transcendentally change the door, or you can simply design it out by constructing a wall, bookcase or other architectural item in the door's place. If, in your career, you find that opportunities almost knock, but not quite, perhaps the way to your door is not clearly marked. The only path may lead to your competitor! Your path must clearly show the way for your benefactors to enter. Your opportunities may come too fast for you to handle if you do not slow them down and get them to smell the flowers on the way to your front door.

Presenting Issue: I feel like things happen too fast. Sometimes I feel hemmed in, up tight or like too much is required of me.

Movement: Standing, begin to sway. Move slowly, without thought of where the movement is leading. Notice what your body does.

Affirmation: Pause. Sit down gracefully. Relax. Feel the affirmation arise from within.

Feeling of Arrival
Feature #4 of the Career Endeavor

Having entered the general domain of your home and meandered toward the doorway to the more intimate inside quarters, the soul seeks a feeling of arrival, something which says, "Yes, you have come to the right place."

You can assist this feeling in your landscape design by making the main doorway clearly distinguishable from other doorways. This can be done with color, trim, or unique hardware. Or you might use a sign with a symbol or words letting people know this is the place where they are welcome.

You might place a bench here because this is the place to pause and reorient oneself, to leave behind the thoughts attached to where you just came from and to begin noticing all the reasons you are glad to have come here. Your visitor, your client, or yourself all want to be shown, "This is the place you have been looking for. You have arrived."

Having stepped beyond the (1) Natural Barrier to enter your domain, you first either notice the (2) Entrancing Gateway nature has provided or the one you have created where all will pass through. Then you invite people down a (3) Gently Winding Path to the place where they can stop for a minute to compose themselves before going inside. I call this the pause at the porch.

If your structure has a porch or one can be built, it is best if it can be wide enough to offer a sitting place and a place to rest packages while finding your key or knocking. It is the place of composure and preparation for the next part of the experience. If there is no porch, what might you do to give the same feeling a porch would give? Are there sheltering trees or could the area be marked off with stones or a stack of bricks to make a seat? Compose the pausing place.

It is the nature of Wild Grace (good household chi) to want to leisurely enter your domain so that she does not miss anything. She loves to bless every stone, flower, bird, bench, and whirligig she sees and thus energize your creative intent. If she comes in too fast, she might feel like a whirlwind or a swift arrow. You would miss the opportunities and benefits she is trying to bring.

Likewise, without a pausing place, when you come home from work or shopping you might drop your keys, stub your toe or miss the beautiful bluebird that just flew by. Give yourself a place to sit your packages down and make an easy transition from outside to in.

Presenting Issue: I feel as though I never quite reach my destination. I do not achieve my goals. I never get anywhere.

Movement: Pause. Sit down gracefully. Experience the moment.

Affirmation: Arriving love-filled, I am always ready for that which is offered before me.

Aura of Authority
Feature #5 of the Career Endeavor

The doorway your guests face before entering should let them know this is the small part of the world over which you have gained command. They are now entering your area of stewardship. The door symbolizes your willingness to take responsibility over your "world." In order to provide a sense that your guests themselves will be well taken care of, your door must exude your authority.

Your own concept and style of authority may be different than someone else's. Therefore, your door might be a finely handcrafted Victorian filigree-embellished work of art or heavy timber planks with iron hardware. It can be the most humble of materials and still, by its color and wreath of dried flowers, show you care about the world into which you and your guests are entering. Your door is like the cover of a book, saying, "This is a glimpse of my work; I am the author."

Once inside, the entrance hall again must welcome guests. The basic requirements of most people upon entering a structure from outdoors are the need for sitting things down and a place to put coats, hats, and outdoor shoes. These hangers, hooks, shelves or racks should be within easy sight and reach. Transition is challenging enough without having to wonder where to put things. Your guests, and, of course, you, each time you enter, are going through a subtle shift from orientation toward the big world out there to the small world within. Make it easy.

Many people meet you for the first time through your career. Your front door plays a similar role. Everyone coming to your front door is a potential business client or benefactor. Likewise, everyone you meet in your business is a potential guest at your front door. What is the face you offer them?

Presenting Issue: No one respects me.   I am always interrupted.

Movement: Stand as if standing up for yourself. Stand to feel your power.

Affirmation: I open the door. I close the door. I am in charge of my domain. Repeat nine times.

Fascinating Spot

Feature #6 of the Career Endeavor

The excitement of entering another's world is heightened when some clue to the potential experience is given in the entryway. Think of creating a Fascinating Spot. It can be something to make your guests or clients laugh or sigh with pleasure, something whimsical or profound. It might be a work of art you treasure or a pleasant view through an arched doorway or a fresh bouquet or a simple crystal hanging in a sunlit window.

The item is meant to be a mood-lifter and mind-shifter. It is easiest to capture the senses with change of light, texture, sound or smell in the entryway. Once captivated, the guest is delightfully opened to the next experience you will provide. I have seen a front hall with a collection of hats, an entry porch lined with potted plants and garden tools, a double-doored entry with a map of the U.S. done in stone in the floor. I have been drawn to collections of books, coveys of angels, colored lights and tables of food. Perhaps the most transcendent experience I ever had upon entering a place was in the house of an artist friend. He opened the door to a room filled with candles alight, pictures of gurus and saints covering every wall and ceiling, and small statues of clowns everywhere. Uplifting music was playing, and cushions in rainbow colors covered the floor. I sat awestruck for an hour! Not an inch of the room had escaped his artistic yet playful touch. The room was filled with chi and grace filled me.

The entire journey from the outer world through your front door into the entry chamber is a promise of things to come. It tells your guests or clients something about your occupation and interests. It speaks subtly of your career, letting others know by your relationship to the environment around you whether you might be someone they intend to support. Never underestimate the power of impressions guests receive when entering your domain.

Inside, your guests hope to learn more from you, to experience the world you are a part of and feel its magic. There is no place on Earth where you have more power to express who you truly are than in your own home. Your own business may come close, but it is limited by marketplace constraints. In your business, you have a chance to offer a particular marketable aspect of yourself; but in your home, you can give some space, even in a very small dwelling, to each facet of your being.

Your living room, like the oldtime parlor, might be the place where messes are "off limits." For many people, there is a conscious effort to put their best possessions in this public area, here displaying the family wealth and taste. But do not be limited by convention.

The beauty of <u>your</u> life may have less to do with things than with spirit. Your front room may be decorated with white walls, meditation cushions and a golden Buddha. Or your public place at home could be the garden room where your prized flowers are the greeters of your guests. I have seen massage tables, desks, dining tables, stone benches, rocking horses, exercise machines and easels all looking completely appropriate in living rooms.

If it has a purpose for you, you love it and care for it, there is no reason it cannot be in your living room space. Bring out the things you cherish. Let them greet the light of day. Wild Grace touches you each time you notice the patina of a furnishing well-used. Beauty comes from being worn by the experience of a life fully lived. Even chairs and couches can tell you this. Bring out your best. Let the beauty of your soul be symbolized at home in your own sacred space.

Presenting Issue: I am bored. My guests struggle to get acquainted. I do not know how to "break the ice" when entertaining.

Movement: Notice where there is most energy in your body. Observe any fascinating spot.

Affirmation: Inside home, my soul is revealed.

Easy Passage
Feature #7 of the Career Endeavor

If you can think of a person as "walking energy," then wherever that person walks, energy is delivered. Energy or life force - the Chinese call it "chi" - enters your house just like a person does. It comes in through the openings in your building and travels down the hallways and passageways through all of the rooms and out the back door, down the hill, and on and on, being carried by the wind through the gaps between the trees and the valleys between the mountains and down the river's course.

I like to think of this energy as a Wild Grace, a gift from the Universe, not quite controllable, but certainly open to invitation. You can make way for Wild Grace to enter, coax her into different rooms, get her to visit interesting nooks and corners, but you cannot force her to stay where it is unpleasant. She is a bringer of blessings and a very sensitive being.

She is the same energy that powers the planet. She is responsible for getting the flowers to bloom and the tides to come in. If you provide a home where she is welcome, imagine what she can do for you. Wild Grace likes easy passage, but not so easy that she misses anything. For instance, a straight and narrow hallway from the front door to the back would propel her too fast, causing her to omit leaving her blessings in other rooms of the house.

Design the traffic flow of your house s that she, or any person, is guided gently to meander through each room, her eye being led by the fascinating spots you have created or the tactile experience of textures along the way. Or call her with the sound of wind chimes or the aroma of baking in the kitchen. She is a sensual being and responds to the most subtle persuasions.

You can look at Wild Grace as a very magical guest, a divine saint, a revered ancestor, simply the life flow, or a potential client. The important thing is to give her a form in your mind so that it is easier to imagine what is needed where in the arrangement and decoration of your home. When the flow is gentle and unobstructed from one room to another, the flow of your life career will tend to be the same.

Presenting Issue: I feel blocked, squeezed and misdirected.

Movement: Walk around, noticing how the space and objects shape your movement.

Affirmation: I follow the flow, exploring each room of my being. I pass easily from one phase of my life to another.

Self-Knowledge

We know ourselves best when we are home alone.

The Seven Features of the Self-Knowledge Endeavor

1. Private Oasis
2. Walls Which Protect
3. Plants, Growth and Flowering
4. Personally Meaningful Ornament
5. Dream-stirring Comfort
6. Devotional Offering
7. Raising the Chi

Private Oasis

Feature #1 of the Self-knowledge Endeavor

Everyone has the need for personal space. The size of this space is not nearly as important as the element of control over one's own environment. You may have your own home, your own room, or just a little corner that is under your control. Here you can get to know your soul.

In order to discover your own unique talents and tendencies, it is necessary to be away from others, out of their jurisdiction, where you can experiment with your own whims and fantasies without fear of criticism. Although having walls and a door may seem at first like the only way to achieve this kind of privacy, a lot can be done with simply arranging furniture to define one's independent territory. Screens, drapes, and shelving units can all be useful.

In a work area, tables or desks can be turned so that no one is "looking over your shoulder." Or you may be able to face a window where your imagination can escape into the world outside. Or there might just be a time of day when the office or house is "all yours." You could even designate certain hours as quiet time, when no one interrupts another in any way.

Whatever room you begin to call your personal oasis, you will find a subtle shift take place in how others relate to the space. Your oasis could be a bedroom, a study, a bath, just an area of a room, or a chair or bed. Wherever it is, decide that this is where you will acquire and synthesize self-knowledge. In this place, provide whatever tools you enjoy using for relaxation and keeping record of your thoughts and imaginings. This may mean having blank journals, audio tape, art supplies, empty space, big soft pillows, a hot tub, a raggedy quilt, or anything else that stimulates your inner private being.

This is your place away from the world. You control the temperature, the light and color, the sound or silence, the style, the feel, and the order within this space. And you can always come here to do nothing whatsoever.

There must always be a place and time when one allows the-world-others-are-creating to fade from consciousness. Though the self is always in relationship to everyone and everything around it, the self is also in relation to the stillness. No matter what spiritual tradition is a part of your life, in order to know the well from which it springs, one must be still.

To find stillness, you need "space." Though we are intensely drawn to human activity by nature, we also need time away in order to replenish our spirit. Whether to study textbooks or to contemplate clouds, we need a place free from distraction.

It is good if even a small segment of time and a tiny area of space can be set aside for this endeavor. It might be a chair on your porch at sunset, a meditation bench near your bed in the morning, the secret spot in the back of the garden at noon, or the bathing tub late at night. This is the time and space when all cares are set aside. Whether you call it such or not, your time here is a spiritual ritual. You are making a temple of renewal, a place of glorious letting-go of all that concerns the public person.

It is in these moments that the self identifies its place in the scheme of things and aligns the energies of your whole being with the source of all life. From these nourishing moments, you will feel renewed and directed each day.

Presenting Issue: I have no place to retreat. I am tired, confused or sick. I do not know who I am or what I want.

Movement: Explore the room physically until you find a spot where you feel most comfortable and safe. Stay there for at least 20 minutes.

Affirmation: I take my space. Stillness comes.

Walls Which Protect

Feature #2 of the Self-knowledge Endeavor

    Walls are to lean on, to shield you, to absorb the offerings of sound, warmth, and decoration. To do their job well, they like to be solid and sturdy. Even if the wall is a shoji screen made of rice paper and wood, its appearance can have the quality of dependable durability which allows you to rest away from the interference of others.

    The worst kind of wall would be one which is devoid of

interesting texture, or pleasing color, perhaps in a windowless room and so close to other walls as to limit human movement. This is an imprisoning wall. If you have any room that feels "close" or confining, look to see if you can break the spell by light, color, warmth, texture, pattern or sound.

To increase light, a window or skylight is best, but lacking this capability, artificial light such as lamps or candles or even a painted-on window will suffice. Light colored paint or fabric, especially cool blues will appear to make the walls recede. Full-spectrum light bulbs are helpful where daylight cannot enter.

If you have ever been in a sauna, you know that the extra warmth of this small windowless room gives it a special purpose and alleviates the imprisoned feeling. The texture, aroma and pattern of the beautiful wood also help. With the addition of music, a tiny room can become an uplifting sacred space, the womb where your spirit is encouraged to soar as your body is freed from distraction.

Walls can be designed to keep out noise, unpleasant views, unfriendly neighbors or intruding animals. They protect cherished furnishings, private work, and your space to be fully yourself. If you paint them, hang things you love on them, and touch them, they become friends. They are the guardians who keep the sacred boundary between you and the outside world.

Walls are often colored with paints and always colored by light. Colors are vibrating energy fields. In this sense, they are alive and have a voice which speaks to us. The sun at midday is the most obviously intense color energy, pulsating, radiating its stimulating life frequency to us. It warms the Earth with golds, yellows and reds. It can do the same in your room.

The sky, on the other hand, maintains its distance, peaceful, unobtrusive blue most of the time, providing relaxation and relief. The greens of the plant kingdom combine the yellow and blue and are alive in the middle ground, offering a pleasant mix of activity and serenity to our lives. Which rooms in your home need walls with these qualities?

In our world of created colors, paint, fabric, and lighting, we use these naturally occurring qualities to bring about the right blend of excitement, warmth, and relaxation in each room of our house according to its purpose. A room where serious study must take place might be done in neutrals that will not distract your attention from your intellectual pursuit. A playroom might be painted in rainbow pastels which help you to feel lighthearted. White walls can provide a backdrop for ever-changing moods created by the colors of drapes, rugs and furniture. Protect your emotional sensitivities by choosing the colors which encourage the feelings and activities you want to enjoy in each room.

There are many excellent books available on color as decoration and as therapy. Here, let me only call your attention to the relationship created between the colors you choose. For exterior building colors, look at the colors already existing in nature around you. Each part of the world has a different combination and intensity of the reds, yellows, greens, and blues of the sun, sand, forest, flowers, and water, and a different mix of colors on the already existing buildings. Compliment these.

Inside your home, your color choices may be guided by architectural style or period or limited to choices which compliment existing irreplaceable furniture. No matter what the restrictions, you can benefit the whole by bringing in colors which interact so as to stimulate the feelings that you want stimulated. This is best done as an intuitive process, bringing in samples and seeing how they look, how they make you feel. Trust your inner senses.

Presenting Issue: I feel overwhelmed, restricted or hemmed in.

Movement: How might your body shield itself from others? Explore movements which shield you from criticism, negativity or unwanted experience.

Affirmation: Having created my boundaries, I find comfort.

Plants, Growth and Flowering
Feature #3 of the Self-knowledge Endeavor

A human being is a biological creature. She is made of the stuff of nature. Like a plant, she grows, takes in food, water, air and sunlight for her nourishment. It is important to recognize one's need for natural objects in the home or office. Without them, you will feel empty, alienated, lost.

There is often a sterile, cold feeling to modern buildings. This happens to the extent that nature is denied. Nature is curvy, changeable, even messy. Plastic, chrome and steel, unembellished, are stiff, cool, impermeable. These qualities can, of course, be altered, and if you want to achieve a sterile or cool appearance for a specific purpose, they are very desirable traits. Know your materials in order to decide their best uses.

Most rooms are a combination of many materials. To the extent that you want a room to promote self-knowledge, to foster comfort and relaxation, you will want to fill it with organic shapes and substances. Use wood, stones, water and plants as much as possible. Allow natural light and encourage nature's sounds, live from your outdoor garden whenever possible. Here among living, growing things, the human being thrives. Here, she will want to settle and stay as long as possible. Here, he will be willing to pause and reflect. You are a part of natural life, and growth happens in relationship to growing, creative nature.

Presenting Issue: I feel cold. I experience some sense of deadness in my being. There are dead trees or plants around the house.

Movement: What materials or qualities of light are nourishing you in this moment? Increase them. Decrease them. Notice bodily responses.

Affirmation: I grow toward the Light; this is my nature.

Personally Meaningful Ornament
Feature #4 of the Self-knowledge Endeavor

There are many beautiful things to buy, but at best, these can only be symbolic of experiences you have enjoyed or people you have known. Truly meaningful ornament must not only generate a desirable emotional reaction in yourself, it must also be created out of the feeling that the experience elicited. For instance, let us say, your child went to summer camp and made a watercolor painting of the swimming pond there. This was a place she enjoyed and found beautiful. This art would be very meaningful personally because of your connection to your daughter's joy and because it was created out of the feeling engendered by her experience.

Perhaps you travelled to the Yukon where you watched a native weaver create a tapestry with the yarn of local colors. Because you were there, this would be more meaningful than if you just found the tapestry in a store. Better yet would be a weaving you made yourself out of found objects and yarn passed on to you from your grandmother. Collages, found objects, revered memories captured in photos or paint, inherited collections, one's own art inspired from within, favorite jewelry or clothes, hand-me-down quilts or toys from your youth can all be used as meaningful ornament in your home.

You may not feel as artistically talented as you would like to be, nor have time to create everything you would like to have, but you can still add your caring energy to the ornament of your home by arranging the items which hold meaning for you in a unique way. A "unique" way is one that only you, because of your individual habits and preferences, would think of. It comes out of your spontaneous feelings when you walk into a room. For example, you can place the chair right where you like to sit, with the table within reach of your hand, footstool right for your feet, and the ornamentation of pillows, throws, plants and pots, pictures, stationery, pens and journals, teacups and flowers, wastebaskets, lamps, slippers and magazines right where you like them. The feather you found on your walk and the stone you picked up at the beach and the beaded fan your friend gave you are each in their own special spot that you gave them, each visible or carefully kept to remind you of those special moments.

As you come to know yourself, certain objects will take on meaning. You are probably familiar with some house of an older woman, perhaps your own grandmother, where photos and mementos of her grandchildren and all of the gifts they have ever given her are displayed on the mantle, or grandfather's woodworking shop may have been a museum of interesting tools. The modern refrigerator door is a place where all manner of creative works are displayed in a spontaneous fashion.

It is the unique interests of the people in the household that give the home its character. When you walk into a house that looks like a photo from a glossy home decorating magazine, it might be pleasant, but it will probably not hold your attention long or make you feel like being there. The order and coordination of fabrics and style might satisfy your taste, but something will feel lacking if the home dweller's interests are not displayed.

You will find yourself drawn to whatever is personal: the books on the shelf, the collection of special stones, the display of family photos, even the cover of a matchbook or the flowers of the day. Your interests do not have to be noteworthy. The collection of prized antique vases is seldom more entertaining to your guests than the bunch of teddy bears you saved from your childhood. The important thing is to give place to the things that have real meaning for you. Your guests want to become acquainted with a real person. As long as they are made to feel comfortable in your home, they will then gravitate toward the carnival of interests you present them.

Arrange this display of self-knowledge in a way that pleases you. The mementos of your life give you constant feedback on how fully you have lived. Your medals, trophies and diplomas may tell of your heroic efforts. Your quilts, baskets and hanging herbs may speak of your love of nature. One friend of mine has a wall of photos of the women in her ancestral family to show the female heritage she carries forward.

If all of your symbolic and meaningful objects are packed away, let this be a self-realization. There may be parts of you that you want to keep hidden from public view or that you fear would be rejected. Or maybe you just do not know how to display all that stuff. If so, begin by considering that you intend to honor the life experiences you have had. Take one set of experiences or period of time and get out some things that remind you of those "good old days." Play around, looking, remembering, arranging until you feel a reverence for what you have been through. Even if there are life experiences or periods that you would just as soon forget, it can bring much self-knowledge and occasionally healing to arrange the symbols of that time in a positive way. Usually, the worst of times has contributed to who you are now as much as the best of times has.

It would be impossible to ever retell each detail of your life story, but symbolic objects, especially those made beautiful and revered, sum it up for you. Polish up the past and you will be shining up your self-esteem as well. Then proudly display your present interests, and everyone who enters this personalized domain will feel the secret person inside themselves cherished and encouraged as well.

Look at the art, knick-knacks and collections in your house. Can you remember a fond event connected to each one? Have some of the once important things lost their meaning? If it means nothing to you, get rid of it. An object you do not like will continually put you in a bad mood, syphoning your energy and thereby affecting your health, your wealth and your relationships. Let go of tired, broken, intrusive or meaningless objects. Keep objects given in love or created with love and loved by you. They will soften the hard edges of life forever.

Presenting Issue: I feel disconnected from life. Nothing has any meaning.

Movement: Decorate your body as you do for special occasions. Use cloth, jewelry, make-up or anything that pleases you. Make the movements a slow, purposeful dance.

Affirmation: The meaning of my life is clearly before me.

Dream-stirring Comfort
Feature #5 of the Self-knowledge Endeavor

Where the body can forget itself, the imagination is freed
to dream. It is dreams that stimulate life. It is dreams that
allow you to experience the possible, to try on courage, to have
the love of your life, to redo mistakes, to take your talents
beyond the limits, to make fun of the mundane.

Let your bedroom be the room where you put your
ordinary self to bed, laying down your burdens, slipping away

from the everyday. Make your bed, whether it is a mat on the floor or a queen size waterbed, the place which by its form and coverings gives you the feeling that it is okay to let go. Maybe it is piled high with down comforters and feather pillows so you can sink into its warmth. Or it could be a futon in a stark white room, empty of clutter, where nothing calls to you but the underlying order of life.

It could be a hammock in a tree or a nook in a trailer where a picture of a guardian angel hangs and reminds you, the world is not all on your shoulders. However humble or magnificent your sleeping quarters, they should make you feel secure enough to relax. They should remind you of worlds beyond the ordinary. Special places. Dream places. Where you can renew and feel home.

Presenting Issue: I have no dreams. I feel restless.

Movement: Make your body perfectly comfortable now. Stay there for one hour.

Affirmation: I dream. I am alive.

Devotional Offering
Feature #6 of the Self-knowledge Endeavor

When a person is allowed to dream, he or she usually finds a source of inspiration. This source feeds the life of that person. In the space occupied by anyone fed from the well of dreams, there usually arises a spontaneous exhibit of symbols of their inspiration. The natural course of events is the spreading of one's inspirational images onto all things in the surrounding material life.

In other words, when you have time and space to imagine, your imagination takes you beyond limitation and fills you with creative ideas that then flow through your words and actions into the outer world, coloring everything you do. The items you produce then become expressions of the beauty you found within.

You can see this in all ancient cultures, from the baskets woven by Native Americans to the temples built by the Greeks. But where dreaming was looked down upon and homes were mass produced, you often see a lack of beauty, a lack of works inspired by the soul. Every place which uplifts the spirit for generations, has been built by individuals as a devotional offering. Mass marketing can generate fads, some quite fanciful and interesting, but only the dream can generate a thing of lasting beauty.

It takes an individual, living life with time to provide for idiosyncratic comforts, to produce something another individual will truly enjoy. Buildings designed to be financially efficient without regard to human preference always fail, in the end, to have provided anything at all. A cathedral built hundreds of years ago or a cottage small, will on the other hand, please the eye in every direction, if built by people who thought of the process as bringing "the Dream" through themselves into manifestation.

Let your space flow from the inspired place you reach by rest and renewal. Devote yourself to expressing the spiritual wealth you realize from your dreaming place. And offer the work it takes to produce the form back to the Timeless Source.

Presenting Issue: I feel disconnected from the Source.

Movement: Form your body into an expression of devotion. Maintain this posture for at least 20 minutes.

Affirmation: My soul continuously expresses the Timeless Mystery.

Raising the Chi

Feature #7 of the Self-knowledge Endeavor

The Wild Grace of self-knowledge is personal chi. As you come to know your needs for rest, activity, stimulation and study, you will provide the space, time and things you need for renewal. Soon you will be noticing greater health and energy in yourself. This is Wild Grace's inner gift to you.

Arrange each day to your liking. Celebrate yourself in time. Do a sun dance, a moon watch, have a room where your spirit can fly. Call it a studio, a cell, a temple, a barn, a greenhouse, a den, a cubbyhole, a womb, a tower, or a cave. Be brave. Build a foundation for future creation. Pile up stones or bones and symbols of the Goddess, or, be more modest. Make a grotto for your auto, a room for your blooms. Open up. Put up stars. Paint a sky. Cover a chair with a bear. Run in place. Eat breakfast in lace. Play cards all alone. Sing and/or moan. Hang all of your necklaces and scarves on the wall. Play ball. Do what you love; self-knowledge will follow. Without these experiments, life would be hollow.

Personal chi is energy to spare, energy to share, energy to care. When your home serves you well, you will serve others. It is efficient, ecological and holy. Do not settle for less.

Presenting Issue: I feel ill, depressed. My energy is low.

Movement: Seek the space and position where you feel most energized. Dance freely.

Affirmation: Enjoying life, my health increases. I have energy for everything I enjoy.

Ancestors

The blood of the ancients flows through our veins, heals us, and the circle of life remains.

The Seven Features of the Ancestors Endeavor

1. Soil, Stone and Body
2. Gathering of Kin
3. My Place Among Others
4. History of Happenings
5. Tradition Honored
6. Tools That Work
7. Death and Decay

Soil, Stone and Body
Feature #1 of the Ancestors Endeavor

There is a foundation your life is built upon. It is the heritage of your ancestors. Their bones and bodies become the soil which becomes the food, which becomes your body. No one is outside this process. Your physicality comes from the lives of others. Your home, too, comes from the soil, the trees and the stones that were once the bones of your ancestors. All life is connected and is, therefore, sacred.

It took a lot of energy to raise you, and it took a lot of toil to build your home. This effort is worth respect. It hardly matters whether you like your home or your ancestors; the important thing is to recognize where you would be without them, and honor the roots of your present-day existence.

If you can find a way to symbolize for yourself the connection between your home, the elemental earth components it is made of, and the people that inspired its style and worked on its construction, you will have come a long way toward establishing a sense of the interdependence of all things. Life is a circle, and home is the place where, traditionally, birth and death occurred...and life continued.

You have not only personal chi, but the chi of your people. Different races and nationalities, tribes, clans and families have a different energy about them. Blended families from differing ancestry also have a feel or a vibration you subtly identify and respond to. What is the energy of your biological heritage? Are they robust, long-lived, musical, fun-loving, earthy, cultured, impetuous?

Whatever their traits, physical, emotional, mental and spiritual, you have inherited them as your foundation. Find a place in yourself where you can feel good about this inheritance. Then make a place in your home to symbolize the meaning this has for you. Let us say, your father and his father before him were carpenters. Could you show a piece of their work by hanging a photograph of the house they built? Or your mother's family all quilted. Do you have one of their quilts on your bed? Maybe your entire blood line was outrageously adventurous. Could you make a collage of letters, stamps and postcards of where they have been? My father loved to gamble. I keep a pair of dice around to remind myself that taking risks is part of my nature too.

Presenting Issue: I have no one to guide me. I did not receive the training I needed for life. I feel shortchanged.

Movement: Massage your body, paying special attention to the shapes of your bones.

Affirmation: I honor the Earth down to my bones.

Gathering of Kin

Feature #2 of the Ancestors Endeavor

In this era of mobility and changing family ways, you may not be close to your biological relatives. Yet, the human need for kinship is very strong. We need others. We need the wisdom of those who have travelled life's path before us. We need the fresh perspectives of youth. We need peers with experiences similar to our own. We need wise elders. We need a human family no matter where we are or what we do.

I suggest you create your own local version. You need a couple of elders you admire. You need a few lively, curious children you enjoy. You need people your age who share your interests. None of these people have to be perfect. You do not have to live with them. But you do have to make a place in your heart and home for them where they can visit and feel comfortable.

Any older person has some light to shine on your life, even though times have changed. History is always a teacher, especially if the person telling her story had ideals similar to your own. What were the trials she faced, the joys she felt, as she made home? What were the struggles and obstacles overcome as he found his true work?

If you do not have your own children, you can sometimes be a very important person in the life of someone else's child. Your home can be the magical, mysterious place that is fun, safe and made special by your unique presence. Your home might be the only place where a child from a large family can receive individual attention. Or, it could be the place where an only child receives the group interaction your larger family can offer.

To welcome the kind of self-created family you desire, think of what kinds of furniture they would be comfortable in. How might it be arranged to facilitate intimate conversation or playful activity? What do you hope will take place between you? How could you arrange your house to make that possible?

Homes are gathering places. The people you gather bring Wild Grace, that is, they bring the energy of life to your home. If you want this energy to be beneficial, make your home inviting to those who have blessings to offer.

Presenting Issue: I have lost my family through separation, divorce or death.

Movement: Lean on someone. Relax into it.

Affirmation: I acknowledge my spiritual family, those friends who support my soul.

My Place Among Others
Feature #3 of the Ancestors Endeavor

Even while we strive to be above the crowd, to make a name for ourselves or to exhibit our unique personal qualities, we still want to be a part of a greater whole. We look for a balance between our eccentric expressions and blending comfortably unnoticed into the crowd. Our homes and workspaces share these two needs.

If your neighborhood is modern suburbia, you may be

looked upon as quite odd if you let your yard grow into weeds and wildflowers even though, if you did so in the country, no one would notice. If all of your friends are furnishing their homes with garage sale bargains, you may not want the reputation that would come from using conspicuously expensive furnishings in your own home. And, of course, we are all familiar with the longing to keep up with the crowd we admire.

You have a place among others. You are in relation to your surroundings. It is good to think about just how you would like to be looked upon by your neighbors. Some of us can handle being the wild place on the block; others are content only when their home blends perfectly with its neighbors. Know yourself and know that the style, color and design of your home will communicate who you are to those around you.

They will send you one kind of energy if they approve of your choices, another quite different kind if they do not. Public opinion is a kind of chi. You may enjoy the waves of appreciation or take pleasure in being the talk of the town. Most people prefer to strike a balance, not wanting to cause outrage nor give in completely to subtle pressures to conform. Find your comfort zone and the energy aimed your way will always feel like a gift.

Presenting Issue: I feel odd. I feel unaccepted.

Movement: Sit in a circle of others.

Affirmation: I have found my place in the overall plan.

History of Happenings
Feature #4 of the Ancestors Endeavor

Every house has a history, even if it is just the time it took to conceive of it and build it. Its history has an energy flow, subtly affecting the future occupant...you. If the previous owner was successful, her state of well-being will have added reminders of prosperity here and there around the house which you will see and appreciate. Small comforts, perennial gardens, everything in good working order, fresh paint, decorative embellishments, and a higher grade of plumbing fixtures are all examples of possible benefits of moving in after a prosperous person.

If the house is new, the quality of materials used, the detail and forethought that went into the plan as well as the craftsmanship and ethics of the builder will all influence your life there. If you have moved into a house where the previous tenant became involved in unfortunate circumstances, physical or emotional, this energy too will affect your life. Unless you are very strong-willed and self-directed, the nearly hidden influences of the past resident will work to persuade you to follow the same course.

Broken doors and stuck windows will activate your crankiness. Inconvenient floor plans will cause you to waste time. Dirty walls and floors will have you feeling oppressed, a slave to someone else. The emotional grief and confusion of the previous residents can be hovering like a dark cloud in dusty corners and stagnant closets.

What you can do about such a situation is clean, clean, clean. Clean with soap and water. Clean with cheerful song. Clean with happy feelings. Clean with ritual intent. Imagine that you are freeing the stopped-up, leftover thoughts, feelings, plans and longings of the prior owners. Visualize their consciousness leaving and get rid of or significantly alter anything they left behind.

Bring your intentions for your life in the home clearly to mind and anchor them there by placing symbols of what you hope for throughout the house. These symbols are handmade prayers which call upon the spiritual forces that be to align with your new purpose for the house. For example, if in your home you hope to create close relationships among family members, you might symbolize this by having pictures of family good times or a decorative theme of hearts entwined or baskets of games all can play.

If your intent in your house is to totally retreat from

work world stresses, you might have minimal furnishings on the order of a zen monastery. Just glance through some magazines until you are drawn to an image. The image will tell you something about longings and ideals you currently hold. Frame the magazine page if you cannot duplicate the feeling in another way.

Have you ever wondered why the homes of famous people become shrines after their death? It is because we love to enter into the domain of creative, powerful beings. We feel that to touch their space is to touch their personal life. Their furnishings, often arranged just as they had them, give off a vibration that touches us and adds to the awakening of their same qualities in us.

Bring a heritage of love to your home and leave this cared-after inheritance to your children. Keep the history of your estate, even if it is one room, and live to pass on a legacy of love and success. Where your own circumstances have not lived up to your hopes, accentuate the understanding that the "misfortune" has strengthened your will toward some other good.

Presenting Issue: My luck has turned bad since I moved here. The house feels cold, dark or negative. Prior owners had bad times.

Movement: Tie a red ribbon on any physical places you have been wounded. Notice how your body has compensated emotionally or physically for any injury. Without beneficial history (that is, where physical or emotional support was lacking), your will becomes strong.

Affirmation: I am a creation of history and will.

Tradition Honored
Feature #5 of the Ancestors Endeavor

We have all, by nature of our birth family and place, inherited certain traditions. You may be a blend of nationalities, races and religions. You may be currently drawing inspiration from another time, place or people. In order to feel connected to the great circle of life, it is necessary to recognize the traditions which have shaped your destiny.

Your home itself may have its own cultural heritage.

The style of architecture arose out of a specific way of thinking as a society and will tend to generate similar thinking in yourself. At the least, you will gain a little understanding of the kind of people who built such structures.

To dwell in the houses of our ancestors is even more powerful than "to walk in their shoes." At physical and emotional levels, we learn how we are the same and how we are different. We can take those parts of their ways and styles of living that empower us and bring them forward into our lives knowing that these ancient ways were the life blood of a people. By valuing the craftsmanship, the environmental sensitivity or the aesthetic sense of those who came before us, we activate these same qualities in ourselves.

You have probably experienced visiting your parents and getting caught up in the family ways before you knew it. Tradition has a life of its own. This is because intent and habit linger in the ethers waiting to direct every unsuspecting person into repeating what has come before.

Sort out the old and honorble ways from the habitual, dysfunctional patterns. You might want to save the tradition of singing carols by the fire but overcome the tendency to have too many drinks to the new year. Each tradition is a force made strong by repetition.

Practices done over and over in a particular place at a particular time actually create a forcefield left in the place even after we are gone. Have you ever walked into a room aftrer others have been arguing there and felt the disquieting energy? Or have you entered your familiar kitchen and known someone else had been there? You set up vibratory fields over time that your body subtly responds to. Therefore, you can set the tone of future events by drawing on traditions you enjoy from old customs, ancient spiritual disciplines or repeated family practices. Loving words, songs, dances, prayers and positive actions of any kind seed the atmosphere for happy future events.

Presenting Issue: I feel rootless. I do not understand why others behave the way they do.

Movement: Use face paint to mark any physical features you feel are significantly like those of your ancestors.

Affirmation: Learning from the past and present, I create an honorable future.

Tools That Work

Feature #6 of the Ancestors Endeavor

One category of items that we very often inherit from the creativity of people of the past is tools. It is often the old-time tool which is stronger, finer and more specifically suited for the job than its modern counterpart (if there is one). Tools that work are, and always have been, created by individual people whose primary motivation was to get a job done in the best possible way. They were not motivated by the need to sell the tool after its invention. It became popular because it worked.

In our homes and workspaces, we need to have the tools necessary to do our work well. Tools need to be placed where you can conveniently reach them. Everything needed to keep the tools in good working order is best close at hand to the tool storage area. In this way, life's daily tasks proceed without interruption and frustration.

Remember that tools are not just the obvious iron and steel things, but also telephones, music, boots, pens and paper, cooking pots, computers, sewing kits, washing machines, diapering tables, toasters, toy chests and rags. Everything that helps you accomplish anything is a tool.

Somewhere in your heart or home, honor the creators of those inventions that make your life easier and more fulfilling. Tools that work are the products of people that cared. Appreciating the tool is honoring the course of creation, the attunement of person to nature's supply and the need at hand. There is no authority over one's life without having close at hand the tools required for taking charge of one's domain. When you are filling a mothering role, your tools may be records of your children's growth, books on childraising, your child's artwork, a footstool to prop up your feet and a cozy chair for the child to share the special times you will have in your home.

Whether the tools of your trade are financial records, wrenches and bolts, keyboards or cupcakes, the objects necessary for you to exercise control over your area of responsibility are very necessary accoutrements to your place of command. Keep them close at hand.

Presenting Issue: I feel handicapped, disadvantaged or insecure.

Movement: Find something which extends the power or range of your body. Experiment with movements using it to enhance your feelings.

Affirmation: The right tools ease my work and make accomplishment possible.

Death and Decay

Feature #7 of the Ancestors Endeavor

One cannot study ancestry without thinking about death. Everything dies. And in some way, all is reborn. Nature shows us this every day. We are temporary forms, but our lifeforce is so intense that we hang on for dear life.

Sometimes we hang onto things which remind us of old and better times. An honoring of the past is good, but a balance must be kept between a stifling grasp and a peaceful reverence. All things have a finite life span. We cannot expect eternal youth, nor that our home and possessions will remain as bright and flawless as the day we bought them.

Expect ageing. Expect decay. Expect change. Life wants to keep turning things over and trying again. Learn from it all. Make a place in your home where this wisdom is kept. The children of the future need what you know. You might make an annual event of telling stories of family history or have a picturebook on the coffeetable of houses lived in by several generations of kin. You may just have seasonal and annual photos of your land or the history of the lot your apartment is built upon. Time passes. Things change. Anything which you can depict through time will teach about life and death.

Presenting Issue: I am angry. I am bothered when things wear out or break. I do not want to grow old myself.

Movement: Walk across the room as if ageing with each step. When you get to the other side, reverse the process.

Affirmation: I let go of all that no longer serves my needs. I allow life to happen.

Wealth

Wealth is the feeling that the Earth will always provide.

The Seven Features of the Wealth Endeavor

1. Place of Command
2. Holdings In Sight
3. Paper, Trees and Books
4. Establishment of Order
5. Information Station
6. Water, Flow and Vision
7. Safe Shelter

Place of Command
Feature #1 of the Wealth Endeavor

In every room, in every building, in every town and nation, there is a place of command. That is, there is a physical location that, by its nature, allows one to take in a view of the whole when you are there. And that location when viewed from a distance inspires a sense of awe or respect.

As a place on the land, it is usually a high place, but not necessarily the peak, for the peak of a hill can be unprotected.

It may be vulnerable to strong winds, or cause primal fear of attack by one's enemies.

The place of command in a building is often a room not easily accessible by the general public. It also may be higher, up a few stairs from the public domain. At home, it might be your private office or the workshop/garage out back or the desk facing the door to the room it is in.

In every room of your home, there is a power position, a place where you will feel most secure and in charge. You may recognize this position at work, but lose sight of it around the dining table. However, if you confront rowdy children there or end up feeling routinely out of sorts at mealtime, this may be the place where you need to rearrange the furniture.

The place of command is the seat where you look toward the major entrances to the room and no one can approach you from behind. When you can see everything going on in a room, you tend to feel more powerful. In rooms where several doors make placement a challenge, mirrors can be utilized on walls facing the power seat so that you can see in all directions.

A higher or more substantial appearing chair also denotes power. The head of the table position is often given to the person recognized as the authority of the family. The "best spot" in the living room is sometimes reserved for the most respected member of the household. Although you may not want to live your life one-upping others, there are times when being in control of a situation is very important. How much more pleasant to be able to command simply by an arrangement of the room than to be verbally aggressive.

In your place of command, you need a chair which is sturdy, supports you upright and is comfortable. It must give you the sense of ease and power you would like to have with your position of authority. A throne is an extreme example.

You may wish to play with this concept when entering into situations where you want to make a good impression, where you might tend to stagefright or shyness in meeting important people or when entertaining influential business companions. See if there is some position in the room that makes you feel more at ease. Also, notice in the course of the event who ends up appearing most in charge and where they are sitting.

Take advantage of the subtle energies that give power to a place. These can enhance your presentation and your position. Even an inch or two higher, lower, closer or farther from the door, nearer to the most pleasant objects in the room or the best lighting can make a difference in how others perceive you and whether or not they will respect your opinions. You may have learned the importance of timing; now learn the importance of placement.

The place of command allows you to feel some moments of control over your "empire." You sit, ideally, protected on three sides by walls, hills, trees or partitions of some kind and view as large of an expanse as you can manage of your world before you.

Every person, even if she is not the head of the household needs to feel in charge of some location, however small. Give yourself and everyone in your family a space over which they have authority. For a child, it could be a bench near the toy box. For a teen, it might be a bedroom overlooking the street where her friends arrive. For grandma, it might be a table and chair next to her shelf of favorite books.

The important factors are: a view of one's domain, protection from behind, and the right to be in charge of a specific area, however small.

Presenting Issue: I have no control over the situation. Others overpower me.

Movement: Find the most powerful spot in the room. Take a commanding position.

Affirmation: I am the ruler of my body and the place in which it dwells.

Holdings In Sight
Feature #2 of the Wealth Endeavor

We each have many things we hold dear, our families, our land, our home, the possessions we have worked for, gifts we have been given and collections of items we enjoy. In order to experience the feeling of plenty we desire, it is helpful to have our holdings in sight.

Those possessions which cannot be before us can be photographed and given a place of honor on our walls. We have things, after all, to love them and use them or to just look at them or touch them for the feelings they engender.

If we have possessions which make us feel sad or poor or messy, it is best to get rid of them. Notice your day-to-day feelings when you encounter different material objects in your home or workplace. Something may be beautiful of itself but have negative memories attached to it; or something else might be ugly in anyone else's eyes, but bring up fond feelings in you.

Give the things you love a place where you can admire them and interact with them. Allow yourself to feel the abundance of life experience they stand for. You need to feel there is an abundance of the kinds of experiences you desire in life. Experiences are attached, emotionally, to things almost as if they had strings connecting them. The experiences we remember are sensory. To gain the feeling that there is plenty of what you want in life, get the things (in pictures or "in person") that you enjoy, and surround yourself with them.

We each have a sense of just how much of anything is "enough." Some people enjoy stark simplicity in their decor, choosing to experience "plenty" of space, air, order, the richness of design in a single piece, the subtleties of color, light or texture. Others love comfortable chaos, feeling abundance only when surrounded by everything they might possibly want to experience.

Where there is bountiful nature surrounding you, it is easy to feel secure. Mother Nature's seeds, nuts, greens and grains provide basic foods without our having to do much of anything except make sure she has space. Trees grow and rocks form and from these our shelters are possible. But, in today's overcrowded and abused landscape, often Mother is nowhere to be seen.

If we are lucky, we have stores nearby and a job which provides income enough to continuously purchase what we need. Many of us, in fact, have so many purchased goods that we hardly have places to put them. If you have children, sometimes their toys alone can fill a 9' x 12' room. The challenge of our present day lives is to discern the difference between plenty and too much.

We need to look at our material created goods, the "things" that fill our houses and know what is truly meaningful to us and, therefore, worth making a place for. We need to also look at our plot of land and see if we have also made a place for Mother Nature to survive. When you have a general feeling that there is "not enough," it could be because you have too much of what you do not need. It is time to take stock of our real needs, which involve living and experiencing, as opposed to the "things" we have been educated to believe will replace them. Make sure you have the things which truly satisfy your soul.

Presenting Issue: I am not sure what I am working for. I do not know my purpose in life.

Movement: Mentally, go through each body part thanking it for being.

Affirmation: Having made a place for everything I need, all that I see I love.

Paper, Trees and Books

Feature #3 of the Wealth Endeavor

In our modern world, we are very involved in collecting paper. Our wealth is designated by numbers on paper. We have become used to this symbolic wealth to the extent that we sometimes forget what the numbers and paper stand for.

Our true wealth is the trees the paper is made of, the ground in which the trees are rooted, the air the trees breathe and the water which feeds them. Without these living entities, we do not exist. Therefore, our first lesson must be to recognize this true wealth and make sure we have plenty of it. Then we can use our symbolic wealth to purchase the other things made of these earthly materials. We balance our accumulation and consumption with participation in Earth's renewal.

The more symbolic wealth we acquire, the more we must create storage space and engage in record keeping. Real wealth - the trees, grasses, rocks and rivers - takes care of itself, if we allow it to be. Human-made symbolic wealth does not. Therefore, in your home or workplace, there is a need for organization and an accounting of things.

Provide storage suitable to the items you are caretaking. This means closets, shelves, bins, boxes, bags or barns. The easier it is for you to tuck your wares away, the easier it will be for you to find a place for greater wealth in your life. Most lifestyles these days require a place for processing printed information. To deal with the influx of catalogs, promotions, pleas, letters and bills which come into your life, create containers that are placed close to the first place you lay the mail down. These are for the initial sorting. A wastebasket and a recycling bin should be among them. Anything that is clearly unimportant and uninteresting to you should be tossed immediately so that it does not take up time and space in your mind or on your desk.

You may want your processing place to have a picture of trees or a collage of your life dreams. If what comes in the mail does not support nature or help your dream come true, get rid of it. For what you keep, there is a purpose and a place. Thus, the space is readied for Wild Grace.

Presenting Issue: I feel overwhelmed by outer circumstances. I tend to go on shopping sprees, but I am seldom satisfied with my purchases.

Movement: While lying on the floor, tense and relax each body part, one at a time.

Affirmation: From plentiful offerings, I choose that which supports my dream.

Establishment of Order

Feature #4 of the Wealth Endeavor

Order means sorting, prioritizing, categorizing. Turn piles into files. You may need a bookkeeping system, filing cabinets, drawer dividers, sets of jars, coat racks, backpacks or towel bars. Each of these items, and the millions of other organizers, was invented to make your life easier.

Spend one day taking note of every time you go to put something away and there is no convenient place for it. Make a list of all the "wish I hads" and get them. The time and irritation you will save is worth this effort, for every time you are minutely frustrated by lack of an easy place to put things the idea that your life is "lacking" grows stronger within you.

Order and cleanliness are best accomplished by making both easy to achieve. Look at your own routines. Are there any material obstacles in the path between your dining table and your kitchen sink? Your front door and the place to hang your hat and coat? Your dressing area and your bath? Move anything in the way of allowing you to bring order and completion to your task.

If there is any location where a mess always seems to occur, observe the patterns there. What is needed to accommodate the piled-up objects? Would a container help, or a hook or a shelf? What would make cleaning up an immediate and easy task?

Sometimes chaos is the result of accumulation. When you look at your "pile," ask yourself how long it has been there and how old everything is in it. It may be time to let go. Pass on all items which are no longer useful to you to someone who will be glad to have them. Stagnant energy occurs where unused objects sit. Get the energy stirring again by distributing the objects, burning or recycling them. Wild Grace and the benefits she brings may be stuck in that forgotten corner.

Creating order gives you a sense of command of your world. Having things be where they can quickly be found again gives you the sense that all of your life goals are also within easy reach. Your environment affects your world view. Change it to change you.

Presenting Issue: My life is a mess. I find myself wanting to be bossy and control others.

Movement: Walk blindfolded through your house.

Affirmation: There is room in my life for that which I love.

Information Station
Feature #5 of the Wealth Endeavor

As the technological societies evolve, information becomes increasingly important. The more we are asked to be a part of the world as a whole, the more we must know about all of its parts and how they can work together. Currently, we are using books, telephones, television, film, newspapers, radio, computers, fax machines and other related technology to see, hear and study the rest of the world.

There is, however, also a need to feel, taste and smell other people, other places. Or something will be missing. To truly know, we must experience fully and as innocently as our minds will allow. Preconceived ideas garnered from viewing profit-motivated commercial television and news media do not give a whole picture.

Therefore, we must include in our information-gathering systems, a vehicle for transporting ourselves to other locations. This means we need a travel budget, a car, and/or some good walking shoes. To truly communicate, we must be there, touching, tasting, taking in the aroma of life, observing with an open mind, listening, paying attention to the details overlooked by 60 minute documentaries and 30 second news reports.

A place is a living entity containing not only people, but a particular skyline and weather patterns giving birth to unique animals and plants which nurture a different kind of human life. The sun, rain, trees, birds and insects all sing a little differently every place on the planet. These sounds combine with music of drums or pipes or whatever local instruments have evolved. The tastes and smells are not only food and drink but soil and sea and the heat on the stones and homes.

There is no way any technological device can accurately offer you the full experience of being in the heart of it all. Yet, it is this heart we must touch if we are to unite the world in peace, not war and competition. The struggle for power over another people or place only destroys the wealth of our planet.

Instead, we must nurture earthly riches everywhere. We must realize that richness has always meant having the unusual, and to have the entire world created in the image and likeness of the modern western technological society is to lose the vast wealth that is extraordinarily different cultures and landscapes and the traditions they provide.

Our true power will come as we personally commune with difference and allow it to inform us. Let the books and films and phones and faxes give us a clue as to who might be waiting somewhere to meet us. But never be fooled into thinking you know a place or its people without showing up to experience what is happening anywhere. Being there is learning. "Seeing there" on television is letting another's eyes watch for you, letting another's mind think for you. Never forget, we each tell a personal story. The network's view may entertain; the well-done movie is meant to move you; but to move into your own full power, you must step bodily into life in all its forms and variety.

Presenting Issue: I am afraid of others. I judge others harshly.

Movement: Place your body in a new environment.

Affirmation: I have touched the places where the stories live, and they have touched me.

Water, Flow and Vision

Feature #6 of the Wealth Endeavor

Wealth has a great deal to do with flow and little to do with hoarding. To "have" a lot of something is not the same as to "experience" a lot of something. What we really mean when we say that we want more money is that we would like the experience of wealth. The experience of wealth is a feeling of flow. It is imagining what could be, and then immediately setting forth to achieve that vision.

Wealth is a sense that you can move forward without waiting and without interruption. It proceeds from a clear vision of something which excites and interests you and flows like water around all obstacles, letting nothing interfere with its true destination.

This is not to say that it is akin to squandering. For vision is a focused, guiding force, keeping you from spending your time, energy and money on other less important things. When the vision of the life you truly want to be living is guiding your efforts and expenditures, you are certain to stay on course until you achieve its reality. Everything you do is building your positive future and there is always, in every moment, something which can be done toward that achievement.

Like water, however, the destination is not only the end of one course, but the beginning of another. The achievement of your vision is like the lake filled by the mountain stream which then pours itself into other streams becoming rivers; and the rivers themselves never holding still until they reach the ocean. The ocean, like your dreams and goals, consists of glistening waves of changing forms that ever nourish our lives.

Somewhere in our landscape, we must remind ourselves of this. Wealth is water, flow and vision. You may be fortunate enough to live near a natural waterway. If you can, situate your dwelling so that the water is flowing gently toward you. If it approaches too hard and fast, it will threaten your well being and a soft barrier must be created, but if it glides and shimmers toward your land bringing feelings of life, energy and peace, the placement is good.

If you only have space for a birdbath or a tiny fountain, place it outside the window where you can see it from the desk where you handle money. Imagine the water is bringing you inspiring vision, relaxation, and wealth. Remind yourself that the wealthy life is the flowing life that streams toward your goal.

Presenting Issue: I feel insecure. There is "not enough." I am always working but never quite seeing what I get for it.

Movement: Dance or slither on the floor as if you are water.

Affirmation: I proceed without wavering on the path to my goals.

Safe Shelter

Feature #7 of the Wealth Endeavor

Wealth cannot bring peace of mind if it is constantly threatened. A luxurious mansion will allow few feelings of prosperity if paying its mortgage is a constant worry. Debt is threat, perhaps more devastating than war or natural disasters, for debt limits freedom every day for as many years as it will take you to pay it off.

Safety is knowing that 1) war is unlikely, 2) disaster

damage can be repaired, 3) your home and goods will probably be in your possession as long as you choose them to be, and 4) your family will, therefore, always have their basic needs met. It makes sense then 1) to live a peaceful life and support peace-making in your personal and political activities, 2) to insure your belongings with skills and/or cash to rebuild, 3) to limit your indebtedness to the period of your greatest earning potential and physical stamina or avoid debt altogether, and 4) to cultivate an attitude of self-sufficiency, continuing to learn and to teach your family the skills of survival, earthkeeping (gardening and ecology), and self-worth.

A person who knows how to prepare the ground for planting food, how to erect a simple shelter, and how to create with natural objects the fundamental tools of daily life will never feel insecure and unsafe. Even if the economy of your country failed or you were lost in the wilderness, you would have what it takes to immediately provide for yourself once again.

Although there is no way to be 100% certain that your wealth will never be lost, there are many ways to encourage the inner tranquility that will allow you to pass through disaster, decay, and even death. Life is transient after all. Enjoy what you have while you have it by living within your means so that your days are spent in peace and celebration, not in worry over bills.

Presenting Issue: I am afraid of theft and disaster.

Movement: Make a hut of leaves, twigs and grasses. Get inside.

Affirmation: Having both skill and wisdom, my wealth is assured.

Fame

Fame is when the sound of your name meets the hopes people hold in their hearts.

The Seven Features of the Fame Endeavor

1. Reputation
2. Observation Places
3. Wind, Sound and Voice
4. Clan of Encouragement
5. Giveaway
6. Obstacles Overcome
7. Pause, Receive Blessings

Reputation
Feature #1 of the Fame Endeavor

Where you live has always been an indicator of position in the community. The right or wrong side of the tracks, the upper or lower part of the landscape, the exclusive north, south, east or west side of town, or a historic district have all carried strong connotations of your wealth and status locally. Whether you like it or not, whether it is fair or not, these judgements are going on in regard to your house's placement every day.

Your neighborhood's reputation precedes your personal individual reputation as people approach your home. It may be that your neighborhood is known for its ethnic mix, its mansions, its crime rate, its historic roots, its clear lake or its toxic dump. You should know what it is known for because its reputation will affect how people see you and relate to you.

If you are living in an area known for its natural beauty and fertile soil, count your blessings. If you are in an exclusive section of town enjoying the privileges of the wealthy, it is easy to overlook the isolation that may be keeping you from interaction with other interesting groups of people, and, therefore, from some of the amazing variety of experiences life has to offer. You may also find yourself worried about protecting yourself from thieves. These are the same problems you might face if you live in a very poor section of town; of course, you will find that in the wealthy section, your image is much better.

Perhaps living in a neighborhood between the extremes will allow you the most creative options for developing an individual reputation based upon who you truly are. However, at every level, there are people caught up in keeping up the appearance that they are exactly like "everyone else." These people maintain the status quo which is the backdrop for your creative expression. They are the greenery in front of which you may flower.

Your home and yard, and therefore you, come to be known in the context of your neighbors' way of life and the general landscape of the area. You have the opportunity to distinguish yourself within this context in any number of ways. By your home's exterior appearance, you can become known as "the house with the blue door," "the tidiest lawn in town," "the artist's place," "the house with the great rose garden," or, of course, in any number of negative ways.

Look at your building and yard from a neighbor's and also from a stranger's perspective. What is the reputation preceding their introduction to you as a person? When they describe your place to someone else, what words might they use? Your place, that is, status, in your local world depends greatly upon your geographical place - your land and home - and the way you care for it.

Presenting Issue: No one knows who I really am.

Movement: Dance the spirit of your "house and yard."

Affirmation: I am known for the way I treat my home.

Observation Places

Feature #2 of the Fame Endeavor

We all like to observe life. Sometimes it will be by watching the birds, sometimes the people or by enjoying the sunset or the changing seasons. Depending upon our mood and the weather, we enjoy watching from different places at different times. We like to feel sheltered and protected when we are in the watching mood, close enough to see, but not so easily noticed by those we are watching.

Usually, people are most comfortable with their backs to a wall. If outdoors, they like to be sheltered by a bit of roof or the shade of a tree and prefer facing the sunny part of the landscape. Orient any porches, decks or patios where you can lean back and enjoy the view while warming your body in the sun. Give yourself at least six feet by six feet of space on any porch or patio so that others can join you easily in a conversation grouping. Less space will not allow you to have company easily. More than 12' by 12' plus three or four feet additional for any walkways through the area will spread the energy too thin. Opportunities for intimate conversation will dwindle and you will have to hold a dance to get close.

Indoors, observing life takes place through windows and doorways. Make sure your dwelling opens onto interesting scenery. If you are too close to other buildings, create a walled garden outside or a window box planter and bird feeder. If stuck with an extremely ugly view, try hanging lace curtains or put up a translucent paper screen which just lets in light.

Try to arrange it so that some windows have distant views. This lets your spirit soar. It encourages refreshing daydreams which are needed to relieve stress. Where windows are blocked from the outside by building walls or large tree trunks or shrubbery that fills the window opening, this feng shui cure can be used. Place a mirror on the outer wall or tree trunk creating a "hole" into infinity.

Your attitudinal point of view regarding life is directly affected by your visual point of view, the place from which you look out at the world. Remove unpleasant obstacles. Screen out ugliness by placing something of natural beauty between you and "the world out there." Open an area where you can observe that part of the world which, from where you live, is most appealing. By doing so, you will connect yourself energetically with "the big picture." You will know yourself as part of the whole.

Presenting Issue: I am uncertain of others' opinions of me. I do not trust people.

Movement: Sit, observing.

Affirmation: I see the world through the windows of my mind.

Wind, Sound and Voice
Feature #3 of the Fame Endeavor

High on a hill in the mountains, we are often moved to sing out, to hear the echo through the canyons as our words are carried by the wind all over the land. Here we experience a moment of power. We are on top of the world and the world hears our speaking and offers instant feedback of our beautiful sound.

To be heard is very important to us as human beings. It

is a part of being recognized for who we are. At home we want to feel that our opinions are a valued part of the decision-making process. We think that if we are good enough or wise enough, others will listen. But it is often environmental factors that create the listening situation.

Obviously, when a room is too noisy and there are many distractions, we cannot be heard. Yet, people are often trying to talk over TV or music or are telephoning in traffic or shouting for attention. Unpleasant noises permeate the modern world. In order to cope with them, we try to drown them out with our own preferable noise or tune them out mentally. This often leads to not listening.

So many people are not listening, it is hard to be heard. Yet your voice is very important. It carries your spirit into the world. It is the first thread of weaving your vision into the earth fabric. Therefore, it deserves a proper place. You must create your own mountaintop from which to sing.

To do this, you give yourself a silent place and time where you and the soft voices of nature can listen to each other. Then you duplicate these conditions as much as possible in your home and workplace where you will be interfacing with others who might listen to your ideas and opinions.

This meeting and listening place might be two chairs around the fireplace, a garden bench near the fountain, or a sunny nook off the kitchen with a table for tea and a window open to the chirping of birds. Communication is whole when nature is part of the conversation. All the wisest decisions include the well-being of our life-giving planet. If she is present in one of her forms, we are most likely to consider her. The beauty of her soft voice will always encourage cooperation if we listen. As we allow her to be our ally in our meetings with others, we will tend to be listened to as well.

Presenting Issue: Others do not listen to me. I am afraid to speak up.

Movement: Make the sounds of your house, your yard.

Affirmation: I listen and I am heard.

Clan of Encouragement
Feature #4 of the Fame Endeavor

There are times in every life that must be celebrated. What are the traditions you cherish? What are the personally meaningful passages you wish to honor in the lives of your family and friends? Every home needs to have room for the celebrations which are important to the family which dwells there.

In many modern homes, one of the primary spaces for

presentation of personal works is the large blank refrigerator door. The place people gather to give support is often around the kitchen table. This is where celebrations of daily life take place. This is the place where creative ideas are nourished by one's clan of encouragement.

If you do not have a place for joyous approval and spontaneous recognition of jobs well done, create one now. To encourage creative brainstorms, there needs to be a circle of chairs and a table where helpful people can be drawn into conversation and plans can be laid out. Each phase of an idea as it comes into being can be symbolized on the refrigerator door or its equivalent, a designated wall or bulletin board.

Let the history of the idea evolve in visual space until the final results are achieved. Then decorate for success. Energize the idea with symbols that inspire along the way, gold stars, lightning stickers, a magnet that says "Yes!" Once the final stage is completed, celebrate.

It seems to be celebrations that bring out the child in everyone. In the holiday season, the whole house may become the decorated hall of festivity. Birthdays usually get some special attention with the eating place adorned and perhaps a spot for games arranged. These types of celebrations give us a chance to create temporary art with childlike glee.

Paper and bright colors, glitter and gold pick up the energy of those gathered because of the spontaneous creative spirit with which these decorations are placed. There is an element of surprise for the guests, an out-of-the-ordinary treat for all. Be sure to allow your family the opportunity to experience celebrating meaningful events with gifts from their hearts. Fun happens when a heart opens and a spontaneous desire to create an expression of its feeling emerges. Allow this feeling to manifest.

Let there always be a place for a spur of the moment festivity. A stash of inexpensive materials, some would-be-tossed-out odds and ends, is always useful. Combine with paints and glue and ribbons, and miracles occur. The heart has a way, when given a chance, of making the ordinary very special.

There is no need to limit celebrations to birthdays and legal holidays. In other cultures, there are ceremonies for baby's first smile, re-naming rituals, moon gatherings and all sorts of folk festivals. A friend told me of a woman in her neighborhood who invites everyone over once a year for the one-night-only blooming of a flower which grows in her yard.

The traditional birthday party is one way of saying, "We are glad you were born; we support your life with us." But, why not celebrate throughout the year the creative turning points each family member passes through. Your celebration place can be a constant reminder that each member of the family is supported by everyone else. Put up drawings of obstacles overcome. Create a space for "failures" that turned into blessings. Show relationships between one member's success and another's. Symbolize how each person in the group was necessary for any one person's success. By continually creating a visual display of the relationships always behind anyone's recognition, you strongly reinforce the knowledge that you are not competing with each other. You are a clan of encouragement.

Presenting Issue: I am not having fun. I am not supported by others. I feel unloved and unhappy.

Movement: Raise your arms, jump, skip and run. Move as if you just received something you have always wanted.

Affirmation: With celebration, I support the people I love. Their joy is my fun.

Giveaway
Feature #5 of the Fame Endeavor

A giveaway is your offering of love materialized in some form for the pleasure and nourishment of others. Many such gifts come from the kitchen, traditionally the heart of the home, the hearth. In every house, there must be a warm center where those who pass by may count on receiving some momentary reward.

As a child, you might have looked upon the cookie jar as

this place of instant delight. Or, it could have been the warmth of the woodstove or oven, or the place where grandma sat and rocked. The giveaway is a small thing. It is a tithe of love for which you ask no repayment. It is the grease to keep the wheel of kindness turning.

Sometimes in modern lives with both men and women holding full-time jobs, the kitchen becomes a fast food stop. Unfortunately, the microwave is never radiating warmth. There is no flame from the electric range. There is no observable crackling fire in the furnace. Grandmother has lost her place in the rocking chair. And a million other plastic and electronic bedazzlements keep us from even noticing the cookie jar. The old hearth is gone.

Yet, I have seen new nourishing places evolve in families who still understand the need for everyday spiritual materialization of love. One mother places "Angel Cards" and tarot decks on her coffee table. Passersby are encouraged to draw a card for fun and instant inspiration. These cards have uplifting words or images on them. You could make your own deck of wisdom on 3 x 5 cards.

In another household, the bathroom always contains booklets of short daily prayers and easy spiritual focusing lessons. I have also enjoyed visiting a friend whose living room was filled with musical instruments of all kinds. Every guest was invited to play at any time. These instruments included simple shakers, jars of beans, sticks to clack, and other homemade percussion items as well as a piano and a variety of strings. Evenings there nourished the soul.

Where is the spot in your home that invites family and friends to play, feast and find upliftment? Do not count the television or computer game center. Passive viewing does not count here. Where is the live interactive opportunity happening, where people touch and look at each other, where people act in relation to each other. The soul is only truly nourished by real, interactive experience.

Create a giveaway spot. Here, place items to be used by all for fun and conversation, art supplies, games, cards, puzzles, musical instruments, blocks, stones, stuffed animals and dolls, snacks, a "toy of the month," cushions, covers, cartoons, a blackboard, a family creation-in-process, a basket of gifts for guests. You name it. If it brings people together, it is the right thing.

Presenting Issue: I feel tense, tight, constricted.

Movement: To music, do a continuous giving gesture from your heart. (Hands touch heart, then reach out, palms up, extending to the world, then return, repeat.)

Affirmation: I am famous for my brand of fun.

Obstacles Overcome

Feature #6 of the Fame Endeavor

Having set your sights on a future potential outcome, you work toward it. But along the way, both new inspirations and obstacles encountered cause you to adjust your course. You get into a project only to find you need a different tool to complete the job. Or you finish painting your walls peach, and someone walks through the room in a pink dress, and you realize what a great color that would be for your throw pillows. Suddenly, you have a new vision and a new project.

End results are fleeting moments, every achievement leading to a whole new concept of what could yet be done. You are an infinitely creative vehicle. So, in order to feel successful, you must not expect it to be a static state arrived at when all projects are complete. Success is just being able to do what you are inspired to do with little hesitation other than needed planning and observing how the idea will fit with what has already been done.

To proceed, you need to gather the knowledge of those who preceded you so that you do not waste time covering the same ground. Then practice or build upon these experiences which others have offered you and add your own unique touch. Your tools, therefore, will include access to a library, public or personally collected, and the basic raw materials for achieving the materialization of your vision.

Give yourself space to work and a period of time to devote to invention. Every home workspace will require its own individualized arrangement of things to offer you the best working environment. With furnishings arranged for quick and easy access to the tools and knowledge of your profession or goal, achievement of positive results will be a natural outcome.

Repair or replace anything that interrupts your movement toward the life you want to be living. If you are stumbling over rocks or toys or boxes, move them. If you are continually catching your coat on a chair arm, change the chair's position. If you curse at the stuck garage door every morning, fix it.

Every stumble, trip, snag, fall, bump and snarl your house causes by its disrepair or disarray will upset your emotional balance and keep you feeling like a failure. Correct these seemingly minor irritations, and you will feel a major difference in your state of mind.

Success is: flowing easily from job to job overcoming the inevitable obstacles life brings by having knowledge and tools on hand so that nothing interferes with your direction. In your home, pay special attention to stairs, passageways and entrances to rooms. If a wall is too close across from a door so that you feel you are walking into it, put a mirror or a picture with depth on the wall you confront. If your stairs to the upper story are right next to your front door, or your back door is directly across from your front door, energy and, therefore, opportunities are passing you by too quickly. The same situation exists if your home is on a hill down from the street. To remedy these situations, place lights, wind chimes, curtains or other interest-gathering objects between the front door and the "too quick" exit. Anything that stops you from zooming in and out and does so pleasantly, also keeps energy and opportunity from passing by too fast.

Presenting Issue: I never seem to achieve my goals. My successes are shortlived.

Movement: Climb. Climb higher.

Affirmation: I am an infinitely creative vehicle, always surpassing my goals.

Pause, Receive Blessings
Feature #7 of the Fame Endeavor

What good is the achievement of something if you do not pause to receive its blessings? This is a good time to notice whether there are spots of relaxation in your home. Is there a window to the sunrise? A warm breakfast hearth? A squeaky clean shower and dressing area? A comfortable work chair? A view of what you are working for? Are the tools you need at hand? Does each spot have a special fragrance? Are the works of art you cherish placed so that you can see them often? What senses are treated in each relaxing spot?

Although mess and clutter come and go, is there always one spot where you can get away from it all? In a busy room, make a path for the eye to a place of peace. Inside closets and cupboards, place an occasional pick-me-up like a photo of a friend, a pot pourri, or a prayer. Arrange your walking path to include pleasant stopovers where furnishings are arranged invitingly, coaxing you to take a moment out.

How have you rewarded yourself for all you have done? If you look through your closets and drawers, there are probably many things you acquired which were once very meaningful gifts. Have you noticed them lately? Is there a new way each can enrich your present life? Does something need display? Disposal? Continue to sort out, day by day, the blessings from the blahs. Soon you will be left with only "Ahhhh's."

Presenting Issue: There is not enough time.

Movement: Do a continuous receiving gesture to music. (Reach out with your hands from your heart to full extension in front of you, palms up. Bring your hands into your heart. Repeat.)

Affirmation: Having made the efforts for which I am known, benefits enfold me.

Marriage

Marriage, like home, consists of boundaries and free space in a comfortable balance.

The Seven Features of the Marriage Endeavor

1. Place To Embrace
2. Light, Warmth and Desire
3. Surprise of Sweet Smells
4. Intimate Nook
5. Inspiration For Two
6. Variety of Texture
7. Luxurious Lounging

Place To Embrace

Feature #1 of the Marriage Endeavor

In most of our lives, there is a need and desire for close, personal relationships. We prefer these to be ongoing, supportive couplings where each person remains both fascinating and dependable. If we choose marriage or committed sexual partnership, we want the spark of romance to stay alive. Even if we have no significant other to surround with our attracting graces, we can enjoy the fantasy of possibility.

166

In every ongoing love and every hopeful possibility, there is an element of fantasy. We would like to be united with the dream lover. But is there a place in your home for such a person to be welcomed? Where is the place which by its arrangement and furnishings says, "This is where our romantic union can begin"?

Your lover's niche might be a victorian style parlor with a velvet loveseat, lace covered pillows and crystal wine glasses on a small antique table near the fireplace. Or maybe it is a bedroom which overlooks the sea. It could be a folding futon in a room with exotic plants and ethnic fabrics on the wall, a basket of aromatic oils nearby for massage. "Whatever turns you on" ought to be your slogan here.

The important thing is to allow some corner of your house to be the fulfillment of your romantic fantasy. Decorate to please and excite yourself. Make a place for the physical closeness of two human beings. Keep the space alive with personal indulgences like fresh flowers or a music box, a poster of your favorite couple or a portrait of your soul. Keep the room dramatic enough that you are not lulled too quickly to sleep. Add nature - plants, water, candle fire, sunlight - for ongoing interest, for nothing hypnotizes like Mother Nature's everchanging forms. In this place, you are the presiding goddess of love. Let the room speak of her preference and her presence.

The bed is usually the place designated for the most intimate embrace of a loving couple. It can serve the couple best if it affords them support, quiet and privacy. Think of the things you and your partner enjoy most in your intimate moments. Have these comforts close at hand.

You may also enjoy commemorating your relationship in this bed room with mementos of your life together. You may wish to create an altar to the God and Goddess to remind you of your deeper love. In any case, remove all stressful objects and reminders of undone work from the area. Take away anything that draws your attention away from your loved one. Supply what puts you at ease. Give yourself room to please and be pleased.

Presenting Issue: There is no romance in my life. There is not enough show of affection.

Movement: Experience romantic movements of your body (flirtation, shyness, boldness, sensuality, etc.).

Affirmation: I welcome the Goddess of Love to my innermost chambers.

Light, Warmth and Desire
Feature #2 of the Marriage Endeavor

Except in hot, desert climates, human beings usually choose to be in the sun. We are drawn to light and to warmth. We are nourished by fire. There is something so alive about dancing flames. Fire kindles our desire. No home should be without all of the elements - earth, air, water, and fire - in their most pure primal form.

Even if your fire must take place in the barbecue grill or

little hibachi on your tenth floor deck, make sure you experience this element often. In lieu of any place for a roaring fire, get as much sunlight as possible and use candles with abandon. Indeed, candles and romance are strongly equated in our minds. Desire is the fire within, not only desire in the sexual sense, but desire for our dreams and future goals, desire for life itself.

We need this basic red flame energy to get us moving. At the root of our primal consciousness, we want to feel the power of a force greater than ourselves energizing us. Somewhere in your home, let the decor be hot and wild, especially if you cannot be where there is a spot of wild nature. We want to know Life with a capital "L." Our native soul wants to dance and drum and run and shout, to be uncivilized with wild abandon. Without places to be wild, we feel cut off from the source.

We can regain our sense of connection to the thundering heart of the planet by encouraging a wild place somewhere at home. Fire, sunlight, intense red, and heat bring us back to our earthy root center. If we want to excite a lover or to intensely love life, we must see and feel the fire.

Presenting Issue: I feel lackadaisical, worn out, overly sentimental.

Movement: Dance to drumming.

Affirmation: Kindling the flame, I dance to my heart's desire.

Surprise of Sweet Smells
Feature #3 of the Marriage Endeavor

Fragrance is something everpresent. We cannot easily close our noses to the smells around us. Pleasant or putrid, they enter into us affecting our disposition. You may have a sweet-smelling flower garden or you might live near a meat packing plant. Which do you think lifts your mood? Somewhere between these extremes are the smells of your home.

A Soul in Place

First check the purity of the air in your house. Is it free from toxic fumes outgasing from synthetic new materials, glues and finishes? Pure air must be the foundation for a healthy life. There are excellent books available to help you choose non-toxic building and decorating materials. There are some products available which diminish air toxins. Outdoor air allowed inside is the most accessible remedy.

All air fresheners try to duplicate the sweet smell of nature. You can bring nature in with foods. Bread, lemons, coffee and your favorite soups and spices give off delicious aromas. Smells become linked with tastes, touches, sounds and sights. The way to sensual delight is to attend carefully to all the senses.

Smells can trigger memories of past experiences, taking us for brief journeys to pleasant times. Treat your loved ones with the fragrances that will live in their memories as the smell of home. Treat yourself to the smells you love, letting your love be triggered by the scents with which you fill the air.

Presenting Issue: I feel lost. I have no sense of home.

Movement: Annoint your body with scented oils.

Affirmation: Following the fragrance, my longing is fulfilled.

Intimate Nook
Feature #4 of the Marriage Endeavor

Eating is more than just putting food in a body to keep it going. At its best, it is communion. It is a uniting of your body with the body of the Mother Earth. It is a sharing of this body with those you hold dear. This kind of sharing calls for an intimate nook.

Make a place where you and invited others can sit cozily and close as you exchange ideas in the shared nourishment of eating. To take in is to taste, to savor, to relish, to blend into exciting combination, not only dishes, but words and ideas. To be a guest of someone providing this opportunity is to be blessed. It is thanksgiving itself.

Make this intimate nook an eating place that encourages intimate ingestion of what you have to offer. Seating that surrounds, cushions thick, colorful cloth, flowers in the sun, sparkling goblets and steaming kettles could all play a part on this stage you are setting. Give it a look of painstaking care, attention to detail and your special flare, so that if you were a guest, you would want to sit there.

Look at the arrangement of all of the seating in your house. Are guests encouraged to look at each other? If not, where are their eyes directed? To improve relationship, orient the seating so that all can see each other easily. Provide items nearby that may spark conversation. The more intimate the room, the closer the chairs can be. Never expect true intimacy from watching TV.

Presenting Issue: No one talks to me. I experience a lack of intimacy with others.

Movement: In a group (or alone looking in a mirror), veil your face so that only your eyes are showing. Look into each other's eyes as you dance.

Affirmation: As we look into each other's eyes, I recognize a friend.

Inspiration For Two
Feature #5 of the Marriage Endeavor

In every couple's domain, there must be room for both to breathe, for both to feel inspired by the space. Your home should provide the opportunity to express your tender, secret feelings. To encourage this sharing, a sense of privacy is important. This can be achieved not only with a separate room from other family members, but curtains, screens or furniture arrangements and sufficient sound barriers.

If family or outdoor sounds cannot be blocked out, often they can be obscured with music. There are pleasant nature recordings that will also do the job. Bring in the sounds you both enjoy. Fill the space with paintings or other art objects you each find inspiring. Perhaps, place a book of favorite poetry by the bed. What are the other things you, in your uniqueness as a twosome enjoy? Have reminders of these shared passions on hand.

You are together for a reason. Why not celebrate your purpose where you can both be reminded of this "big picture." You might create a collage headboard for your bed with photos of the many places you have been or the children you have fostered or the experiences you have enjoyed or the spiritual focus your life has together. Whatever you do, do it for the two of you somewhere in your home together.

Presenting Issue: We have no privacy as a couple. There is a lack of closeness in our relationship. I have no close relationship.

Movement: Dance, inviting another to join you.

Affirmation: Having come together, a greater gift than either alone could give is given to the world.

Variety of Texture
Feature #6 of the Marriage Endeavor

Romance is a feeling. Feeling is a sense activated by touch. Make sure you have plenty of variety in the touchable items you use to decorate the rooms where you want people to attend to feeling good.

A silky comforter; a soft, velvety chair, a firm mattress with fresh, clean sheets; a slick, polished tabletop; gnarly, handwoven baskets; crisp lace; cool, glossy ceramic tile, and warm, smooth wood are a few of the limitless possibilities of textures you can bring together to stir feelings.

Not enough variety in texture will make you feel cold, as if you are visiting a hospital waiting room. Too many textures and you will feel overwhelmed, a little nervous or distressed, such as when you enter a child's room the day after a holiday gift exchange. Your goal is to have just enough variety of texture in each room to suit its purpose. Every item, small or large, should make you feel the way you hoped to feel in a room designated for its purpose.

The kitchen might be spicy, decorated with orange and yellow and "hot pepper" lights, the bedroom subdued with simple nature colors and cotton cloth, the living room formal and serene with Japanese silks and lacquered wood, and the bath as outdoorsy as a mineral spring with plants everywhere. Or, the kitchen might be a misty blue because you prefer to breeze right through it, the bedroom wild with jungle prints, the living room blended old and new, and the bath with mahogany bookshelves and an antique tub. Create a home that gives you the feelings you have enjoyed in other places or other times. Visiting another room may become as exciting as touring another country, or inspire you to do both.

Presenting Issue: I feel confined, dull and bored.

Movement: Explore textures with your body.

Affirmation: A world of possibilities is at my fingertips.

Luxurious Lounging
Feature #7 of the Marriage Endeavor

In what kind of setting do you feel most pampered? Some people like a big bathtub with a leaning cushion, bubbles and a reading tray. Another person may adore a sauna with thick towels and a huge pottery mug of water. To yet another, a lawn chair on the deck with a wading pool to soak one's feet is pretty close to heaven. Make sure you and your partner each have a place where you feel richly rewarded for the energy it takes to be in relationship.

Conjure up the image of the lifestyle you dream about (even if you do not want to live it every day), and give yourself as many of the accoutrements of that lifestyle as you can pull together. If you can step into your own healing reality a few times a week, you will find your satisfaction with everyone and everything deepening.

If Christmas is your favorite time of year, why not have a "Christmas Room?" Put up the colored lights. Wrap some gifts for each other. Celebrate the birth and rebirth of yourselves and the seasons any time of year. Maybe as a child you imagined yourself as a princess. This can be your excuse to buy a queen sized bed and decorate it with a velvet drape and gold tassels. Put out a satin pillow for the prince and two golden goblets for your potion.

Where did you meet your loved one? Perhaps you could recreate the theme of the place where your love began. Or generate a new dream together. Think of your shared room as a womb of what you are trying to create together. Make sure your partner loves it there too. If the magic is missing from your relationship, perhaps it is only that the rooms where your relationship takes place are dull. Get a little fantasy going and make it happen in your environment.

Presenting Issue: I feel overworked. I lack joy in my life.

Movement: Imagine. Feel the effects of various imagined environments on your body.

Affirmation: Anywhere I imagine, I can be.

Children

It is never too late to be a child.

The Seven Features of the Children Endeavor

1. Creative Play
2. Room To Roam
3. Shifts and Transitions
4. Interests Indulged
5. Cozy Place To Listen
6. Secret Treasures
7. Illumination

Creative Play
Feature #1 of the Children Endeavor

In each of us, there is a child. The child fantasizes one reality after another, creating and destroying possibilities without restriction. Some of us, upon growing up, give birth to or adopt into our care, a new child separate from ourselves. This human child continues the process of playing with realities right before our eyes.

Every child, whether within or alive as girl or boy, needs

plenty of opportunity for this creative play. A child is interested in worlds and only slowly becomes ready to handle the details of those worlds. In other words, a child wants to get involved in the creation of the whole. Miniature towns, building blocks, sandboxes and dollhouses are all tools for the creation of whole systems. Blankets over chairs, cardboard boxes, piles of dirt, puddles of water become cities, caves, roads and rivers as the child is allowed the opportunity to create his own version of home.

The child naturally wants space for a place that feels to her like home. It may be in a hidden corner of the living room, satisfying a longing to be near others, yet with a comfortable personal distance. It may be high in a treehouse at the back of the yard. Wherever the child feels best, she (or he) will create her personal home.

Give your own inner child and the external child a place to play with worlds, to create and destroy without consequence. This practice equips the child to eventually situate himself in the actual world. She learns through play and fantasy which roles are most appealing to her. Within this world one must find a place of one's own, a place for one's individual world to coexist. The shaping of this place begins in childhood. Provide easily moveable parts which can be both created into your child's "playhouses" and destroyed without consequence. Creative play is dependent upon destruction without cause for alarm in order to really fulfill the psychological and spiritual need to fantasize again and again types of places one might want to create for oneself and types of worlds one may want to inhabit.

Life is an enthusiastic, determined, energetic power trying to display itself in magnificent spurts of energy. This unconscious force is always synthesizing its surroundings and experiences and trying to express a counterpoint to them. Some amazing, never-ceasing part of each of us tries ongoingly to deal with the whole of what is happening within and around us. If this force is not strangled by physical, emotional and mental restrictions, it produces art, invention and magic.

Let there be somewhere it can fully happen. This may be a place to sing off key, to hang by your knees, to paint purple panthers, to combine unlikely ingredients, or another way of turning the ordinary world upside down, inside out, and ending up with a new creation.

What if the living room were in the place where the bedroom is? What if the tools were in the kitchen? How would it be to sleep in the dining room? Could the bedroom become a studio? Could the library be in the bath? How about a bed by the fireplace? A table under a tree? What if there were a door where you always wanted it to be? Cleared tabletops and blank walls, empty canvas, space... you must give your child a place in which to freely pour forth the life forms wiggling to get free.

Presenting Issue: I am afraid to make mistakes.

Movement: Wiggle and squirm. Make strange noises.

Affirmation: I build. I destroy. I rearrange. I make change. Thus is creation.

Room to Roam
Feature #2 of the Children Endeavor

Freedom is space to run until you are tired, walk until you feel like sitting, sit until you become fascinated by what is before you, remain undisturbed for as long as you are engaged, and rise up when you are inspired to act. The creative child in you and the physical children in your care need room to roam.

To wander is to dream. Dreaming and bodily rhythmic movement are necessary parts of the creative process. The creative process is the prime mover of evolving life on Earth. Without it, life would grind to a halt. The human race begins to die in its own pollution as the true creative urge is squelched in our society.

There have been inventions and discoveries already made which would allow us to run cars without gasoline, heat homes for no cost, process waste without chemicals, and overcome all major diseases, even cancer. But financial interests have overriden the good of the whole. We know this must change.

In spite of the practice of taking children at their most lively and experimental phase of development and, in effect, chaining them to school desks, some of us have managed to keep our creative spirit alive. It is natural for human beings to want to solve problems for the good of the whole, but in our money-based society, we have reoriented this creative urge, channelling it toward the attainment of personal monetary wealth. Now, as we see the negative effects of this money focus, we are rethinking our values.

If our inner wiggly, squirmy child is strong and stubborn enough, she (or he) manages to make a living _and_ to create a life. She finds a situation where sitting at a desk and counting money or shuffling paper takes a back seat to moving, playing with possibilities, and engaging her spirit in the real dance of life.

Give yourself and your child a place to roam without fear, jump without bumping her head on the ceiling, fall where she will pick herself up, and learn through a freedom of movement to express her full body's needs and feel her full body's pleasure.

Presenting Issue: I feel restricted and confined.

Movement: Crawl.

Affirmation: I indulge in spontaneous rethinking of anything that limits my good.

Shifts and Transitions

Feature #3 of the Children Endeavor

As we create, we change. Change is creation, the opening of new doors and the closing of others. In the externalized structure of this eternal truth, our houses change not only as we traverse from room to room, but as we grow from protected infancy, through active childhood, into experimental adolescence, responsible adulthood, and blessed old age.

Our buildings should let us know by their design that each stage of life, each transition, is okay. We will be safe; our needs will be met; we will have the opportunities we desire. Every hallway, the places which mark our passage, should be interesting in itself. This tells us life is here and now even "in between" larger events.

Every door should open without obstruction onto an interesting scene. This subtly lets us know, everyday, that wherever we go, something we might enjoy awaits us. From every window, there should be a view. The view, if not to distant beauty, should be a microcosm of the world we wish to be a part of. Looking out at one flower vining up a brick wall or a few blades of grass breaking through a concrete walk can tell us more about the indomitable life force within us than acres of formal gardens.

Even in your child's playroom or your own area of creative chaos, the shape of the space, the colors, the dance of light and shadow, the patterns made by places of wear or repetition of things can be enhanced to give an overall feeling of pleasure being there. Look with fresh eyes at all the places in and of transition in your home. What is the art trying to happen there?

You might create a place to honor each stage of life: a cabinet of dolls and baby pictures, a place to climb and discover your body's skills in the yard, a lover's bench, a mother's rocker, a father's woodshop, the wise woman's reading room, grandpa's pancake and juice bar. There is something fun and childlike in every age. Only the toys and our bodies change form. The playful, creative urge is infinite.

Childhood is a time of sprouting. Growth is fast and visible. In the child's world, therefore, it is good to have examples of this natural growth time in view. Small container plants bring growing friends into the child's world, showing her the way of life. The message you want to impart is that everything grows and changes. If we care for it, it becomes a beautiful flower and eventually provides nourishment through its fruit, the offering of its form as food for others or for the Earth itself. This is the natural cycle.

The child is the seed of the parents, planted in the fertile soil of home. Growing up in a nurturing environment, the child will someday blossom and begin giving back to the Earth her wisdom, caring and the fertile soul of herself.

Presenting Issue: I am afraid of growing old.

Movement: Skip.

Affirmation: I travel the circle of life, playing with every age.

Interests Indulged
Feature #4 of the Children Endeavor

Whether you are four or forty, you need a place to indulge that one compelling interest you have discovered. It may be gardening or collecting hats, making mudpies or cooking quiche. As you come to know this individual quirk that makes you want to learn everything about this subject, stomp your feet and scream until you get to have what you need to continue this "irrational" pleasure.

You have been given as a gift to the planet in order to bring Mother Earth the individual uniqueness of yourself because this, somehow, balances the whole. How this Greater Creation works is not important to understand. What is important is that you are a part of it, meant to be who you truly are and not a clone of society-at-large.

Take a space for those "senseless acts of beauty" and those odd hobbies and pastimes of yours, and give a space for the same to all who dwell in your house with you. The fishing gear quarters, the rock'n'roll room, the toys-that-go-toot closet, the condo for cats; who knows what you will come up with. If it is you, it will probably not be "designer labeled." It may not make the better home glossies, but you will feel wonderful there. And where you feel wonderful, wonder will grow.

Say you want to meet Santa or Prince Charming. Collage a picture of those who carry this essence. Make a picture of the gifts you hope Santa will bring or set up a throne for the prince, and place your silver slippers nearby. Buy a dollhouse and furnish it to your heart's content. Get some modeling clay and shape the world you have always wanted. Take that old dresser and paint dancing cows on it if you wish. Give yourself permission to wish upon a star, save for a secret vacation, store licorice in a jar. Be more foolish than others think you are.

Presenting Issue: I feel unappreciated and stifled. I am afraid to look foolish.

Movement: Make unusual faces.

Affirmation: A silly act reveals a soul intact.

Cozy Place To Listen
Feature #5 of the Children Endeavor

The child, internal or external, needs a place her (or his) size, where her body is cradled by the just-right proportion of chairs, tables, bed, utensils, and tools for play. A chair too tall which leaves your legs dangling makes you feel small. A cup too big to hold makes you feel clumsy. Your own things must be sized for you.

Here where your body feels comfortably at home, you

can begin to listen to the more subtle voices within you. Here, you can read, study, contemplate and imagine. Here, you can relate to the physical world without challenge. This could be the place where stories are shared, with pillows, books, music and art supplies for the inspirations that arise from this quiet, but not silent, place.

Listen too, to the unspoken needs of handicapped others in your household or acquaintance. They need places where they can feel that they are right with the world. Access to information, goods and opportunity is something we can easily take for granted. Make sure your house can speak the language of a loved one who is different than you.

Presenting Issue: I find it hard to make friends.

Movement: Cuddle and rock.

Affirmation: For you I make a space just right and tuck you in my dreams at night.

Secret Treasures

Feature #6 of the Children Endeavor

What were the special treats of your childhood? Do you remember any hidden places or stashed treasures, perhaps in the back of your closet or out in the yard beyond the wild place, or the box of buttons or cards or cookies that grandma would pull out for you when you visited?

Everyone needs a treasure box or a place to safely keep the items which have taken on magic. It is the times when life surprises us with good, when we are swept away with love, or when the best in us is suddenly brought out by a situation that we begin to believe in magic, the out-of-the-ordinary happenings of life.

Although we cannot be completely in charge of miracles, we can set the stage to allow for their possible occurrence. To do so, we need to collect some good luck charms. Even if you no longer believe in magic, set your doubt aside. This is the Children's Section, the place of honoring that small, wondering being that still awaits the fairy godmother or hopes for a lottery win. I only ask that you leave at least a tiny increment of possibility open to "it could be." Sometimes, this is the only place for happiness or healing to sneak in.

So get a box that looks curiously special, or design a cubby hole or secret hiding place where nothing but tokens of happy events are kept. A good luck charm can be anything from rice thrown at a wedding to the hood ornament from your first car. If you have what you call "power objects" from your spiritual journey, these can be revered here too, for are we not "to be as little children" in our spiritual devotion, and come with innocence bearing our tokens of love?

Things are connected by vibrations to an occurrence, a place, a time, and a feeling. Each item, therefore, holds some essence of that good time, and acts like a magnet to draw similars to itself. You may look at this as "make believe," but making believe is always the beginning of any new reality. When you imagine, you image-in what is to come. Here in your treasure box, your collected items remind you of times when, clearly, spirit was here.

Presenting Issue: There is no more magic in my life. I long for days gone by.

Movement: Hide.

Affirmation: The Great Mystery is all around and here in things that I have found.

Illumination

Feature #7 of the Children Endeavor

The light in your home can come from children, from creative activity and from candles and lamps. String up lights in gay colors or shine a lamp toward the ceiling, anyplace that is not appealing. The bright idea, the brilliant deduction, the light-hearted smile, the illustrious guest all raise the chi of your home. Shine. Polish. Shimmer and glisten. Make light of the darkness. Anywhere. Everywhere. The brighter, the better.

Illuminate your home. Your soul wants to shine.

If you are feeling in the dark in a certain Life Endeavor, look around your house for dark corners. Lighten them up. Anything from playful rearrangement to a higher watt lightbulb will do the job. The eye is drawn to the lightest part of anything. If you want attention to go to a certain area of your home or your life, make it light.

There are times for retreating to a dark, comforting womb: on a hot or stressful day, to sleep or when you are ill, but for work, play, creative inspiration and general upliftment of your spirit, light is called for. Homes oriented toward the south receive an abundance of natural light, but any room can be improved with electric or candlelight. Full-spectrum lightbulbs are helpful where natural light is severely limited such as during the winter or in interior office space. Give your being the light it needs and you will find yourself more enthusiastic about life.

Presenting Issue: I feel in the dark about things. I seem to attract shady characters into my life.

Movement: Let your head hang upside down as your body drapes over a chair. Look at the ceiling.

Affirmation: In the Light, I find delight.

Helpful People

Benefactors and mentors are gathered by the energy of complete abandon with which you pursue your task. It is because of your focus that their approach is almost always a surprise to you.

The Seven Features of the Helpful People Endeavor

1. Readiness Meets Opportunity
2. Cruising and Courting
3. Easy Stroll
4. View From the Mountain
5. Traveller's Eye
6. Correction of Misuse
7. Beneficial Relationship

Readiness Meets Opportunity
Feature #1 of the Helpful People Endeavor

The full-fledged idyllic life is not a destination that is ever totally achieved. The creative spark in us is too alive for that to ever happen. Instead, there are many "moments of arriving." These are the achievements of well-defined short-term goals, the visitations of Wild Grace, the times when all-of-a-sudden you realize you are, for this instant, really living your dream. You are captivated by a momentary contentment.

Then, the very next thing that happens is that you want to do something else, to mend another broken thing, to produce another work of art, to surpass even this success.

We continually head out from where we have come toward what we think could be. Knowing this, we are wise to enjoy each part of the continual process of dreaming, departing from our state of contentment, arriving at another, dreaming, again departing, and arriving once more. This inner journey is accompanied by the outer journey. We are home, we leave home, we seek home again.

We are readiness seeking opportunity, and this opportunity is found in the larger community of which we are a part. Home is the dreaming place, the protected, supportive environment for your solitary contemplation. As your dreams take shape, they inspire you to a state of feeling ready. You want to move out into the day, into the marketplace, into the world, into the excitement of blending with the whole.

This readiness phase needs a place. It has traditionally been the town square, the plaza, the promenade. It is where cultures meet. It is where people of different lifestyles, backgrounds and interests pass each other closely enough to be stimulated by their differences. The best meeting places feel both exciting and safe. This cannot be a shopping mall, for these have designed out the unusual merchant and taken away the ever-changing natural world of light, shadow, wind and weather. And though people of different cultures may pass each other, they do not interact. When we are in our state of creative readiness, we need safety <u>and</u> difference. We need the excitement of nature and the stimulation of people who live differently than ourselves.

As the world is made more accessible by speedy transportation, we have moved these stimulating gathering places away from our towns and out to foreign lands. We must travel the skies and oceans to reach the stimulating place that used to be down the street. Anyone who has spent hours in airports, buses and trains knows that the fun is not in the "getting there." The opportunity our creative nature is looking for is usually found in the town square of some yet unspoiled city. We arrive, have a wonderful time, then travel halfway across the world to go home, not to have another adventure until our next two week vacation.

This is not as it ought to be. It is time to realize that we must stop undermining our own centers of interface with people different than ourselves. Differences produce the song of life. We need not only other cultures, other races, other religions, other styles of life, dress, food, other sounds and sights, but other lands and other creatures. We need the "not me" to make life interesting.

It used to be that you could drive from state to state or town to town and catch a significant glimpse of life lived another way. Now, you can travel the United States and many other countries of the world and find the same shops, the same architecture, the same goods, and people dressed just the same. As technology spreads the lifestyle of consumer goods marketing, the world becomes bland. As any good cook knows, you cannot expect to delight the senses by throwing everything into one pot and stirring it together. As our towns become less distinctly "ours," belonging more to multi-national corporations, they begin to look like Everywhere Else. Everywhere soon feels like Nowhere, and we have lost our place. If, when we arrive in foreign ports, we continue to change them into replicas of our own country, we shall suffer a great loss. We must then travel farther and farther to find uniqueness and to satisfy our adventurous spirit.

When everyone is thrown together without concern for place, the music of differences becomes a chaotic blend, deafening to our ears, a bitter brew that is tasteless, a sight which no longer satisfies. We must shape our towns and countries as we shape our carefully crafted wares. Even though we are satiated at the superficial level with an overwhelming quantity and blinding display of mass marketed merchandise in the malled city, we remain hungry, our souls starving for the richness of true diversity. We long to hear the song of a single bird, to touch the dewdrop on the succulent leaf, and to walk in the undisturbed silence that is nature without cars. We long for old time Main Street, exotic islands, undisturbed beaches, distinctively different cities, the taste of something truly "other."

Yet we must only reclaim Home. We must recreate the opportunities for creative interaction that are so necessary for the dreams of the human race. Our lives need a harmony of differences, blending well. We are enriched by local businesses whose architectural design is based on local resources and in keeping with local natural beauty, whose merchandise is produced by local workers out of their own creative lives.

In your home town or community, support the local place where different ethnic and lifestyle groups can pass, look, speak and touch safely outdoors in nature's presence. In the best of situations, you will come upon a place where your world, the neighborhood you live in and its lifestyle, meets the strangely different world of another lifestyle group. It might be the boundary between country and city, or the place where rich meets poor, or the different architectural and cultural milieu of another ethnic group. Where the edges of the two different groups meet, there is tension. This tension can be exciting or dangerous, perhaps a little of each.

If there is a neutral zone, where the inhabitants of each area can feel they are both welcome, danger diminishes. Where there are protected places to sit back and simply observe, such as sidewalk cafes or park benches, the strangers provide endless fascination for people-watchers.

Where can you go in your town to comfortably come close to people different than yourself? Look for ways to enable different kinds of people to meet at the borders between their usual realities. This meeting provides much of the excitement of life. Go there in readiness to experience opportunity. Be open to a moment's fulfillment. Be open to the expansion of your dream.

The inspiration and renewal generated by these encounters can come home with you in the form of a fresh outlook provided by someone you met, tasty food from the farmers' market, beautiful ojects from the craft fair, a good story to be retold, tips on how to grow a better garden or just the feeling that home, at last, is the best place of all.

Presenting Issue: I am discontent. I blame myself for not being happy, feeling I should be thankful for what I have.

Movement: Take a long walk to the edge of the familiar.

Affirmation: At the border of my world, I meet exciting possibility.

Cruising and Courting
Feature #2 of the Helpful People Endeavor

In the car-centered world we currently live in, "cruising" is an activity which gives those looking for a safe meeting of others a way to unobtrusively check out the scene. In the days before cars and also in places where there are no cars, this cruise is accomplished in the promenade.

People have a need to display themselves to each other, to present a surface view of what each has to offer the other and thereby encourage relationship. It is a courting behavior. In business, it is called networking. There are unspoken rules about it which one learns, limits which keep you from seeming to be "on the prowl" to encouraging you not to be a "wallflower."

The key to the cruise or promenade is movement. You are not to spend too long in one place. The area where the cruise or promenade takes place, therefore, must have a somewhat circular traffic pattern so that you are able to pass by the same persons more than once. The traffic pattern must also be slow enough so that you can look without bumping into someone else.

The promenade, therefore, often takes place at a central location, around a square, or on a few slow traffic streets where there are shops, sitting places, and a lot of "reasons" to be present. Without this meeting place where people can just walk without being suspect of ill-intent, a town loses its ability to bring people into beneficial relationship with each other.

Discover where the cruise or promenade is taking place in your town. Is it just for teenagers in cars or is there a place where all ages can mingle and get acquainted? What could you do to facilitate the creation or enhancement of this important hub where people from all directions will naturally gather?

Presenting Issue: I am shy. I find it hard to meet others.

Movement: Take a walk with the idea of presenting yourself. Strut your stuff.

Affirmation: Circling around the center, we do the meeting dance.

Easy Stroll

Feature #3 of the Helpful People Endeavor

As cities continue to expand with little regard for quality of life, we lose more opportunities for enjoyable short walks to anything. Cars are convenient for long trips and necessary to deal with urban sprawl, but we lose touch with Earth when we do not touch her.

Something should be within an easy stroll from your home. It might be a nature spot down at the end of the road or a neighbor you like to visit or the post office or the corner grocery. It does not matter so much what you are walking to as long as the walk is short and pleasant enough to make you want to do it.

Along a good walk, you will encounter blossoms in the spring, birds collecting berries, children playing, the dance of light and shadow from the overhanging trees, a person or two who will say "hello" and the continuing slow changes of nature as she does her seasonal grooming. An easy stroll is effortless exercise for the body and balancing medicine for the heart and soul.

Helpful relationships begin with repeated friendly encounters with other human beings. The more people see you around, the more they accept you and are unafraid. If you can work near home, you see what you are working for every minute of the day. You work alongside your friends and loved ones. You feel connected to your neighbors because you have a common purpose, building a safe and pleasant environment in which to play, grow and rest. You are surrounded by others, if everyone works near home, who are also creating a world in which you might all have a chance for abiding in happiness. The stress of long, traffic-filled driving time, the expense of commuting, the lack of instantly seeable results of your labor, the feeling of isolation and alienation, the manufacture of meaningless and even harmful goods are all avoided by working near home if home is a place you love.

The more humans are daily uprooted and isolated in windowless containers chained by the clock and wage to uncomfortable chairs with views only of computer screens, the more they will need addictions to survive, for addictions feed on separation. Addictions substitute for life. There is, indeed, a place for technology, industry and pleasures of all kinds, but that place can never replace home. It is only after home is established and alive with purpose that a sense of celebration will be our natural state. Work as close to home as possible, and if you cannot, make home wherever you are. Treat your car like a house. Treat your office like your room. Treat your client like family. Be a good neighbor on the bus. Apply all of the principles of the nine life endeavors to every space you occupy. For the good of your soul.

Presenting Issue: It seems as though I spend half my life in a car. I am out of touch with friends, family, neighbors and nature.

Movement: Greet someone on the street. Pay attention to your body in the greeting.

Affirmation: Engaging life at every turn, happily I wander.

View From the Mountain
Feature #4 of the Helpful People Endeavor

A town which gathers people in relationship, as opposed to a city where the streets are full of people never meeting eye to eye, is a town where the surrounding scenery is pleasing. People enjoy flowers, trees, fountains, interesting views, and artistic creations. People do not enjoy 20 story slabs of concrete, wall to wall asphalt, parking lots, noise, and garbage. One would think this is obvious. Yet, construction goes on, paying no attention to what people enjoy.

People are relatively easy to guide. If the sidewalk leads them between tall buildings, they will follow it. People have destinations - home, shopping, work, school - and they will usually take the shortest route, but the experience of that route can put them in a good mood or a bad one. The state of mind they arrive in at the end location can be greatly improved by a pleasant journey getting there.

Notice the route to your home or business and to the routine places you must go each day. What is the scenery that nourishes you each way? Is it protected from the destruction called "development?" How can the most-used ways to town be made more scenic? How can what is left of nature's beauty be protected?

Sometimes we get so caught up in the details of daily life, we cannot see the forest for the trees. We do desperately need to see forests, to see all whole interdependent systems and to stop acting as if every place and every action existed in isolation.

You cannot so easily bury a stream once you have observed the river in its course to the ocean, seen all of the fields it watered, plants and wildlife, crops and livestock that it has nourished. You cannot so easily build a highway through the center of town if you have looked lovingly at the shape of the land and the integrity of roads and houses shaped by the land.

It is necessary at times to take the long walk up the mountain to let the soul see how far you have come and what is left yet to do. The high view asks for self-reflection, inspires new vision, and always reminds us how small we are compared to vast nature. The view from the mountain tells us instantly where we have gone wrong and perhaps what to do. It is an important spiritual event.

Go to a high place. Observe. Notice how it affects your life. If you can, create a high observation point from which to see the whole of your own land. A ladder to the roof might do it or a perch in a tree. Give yourself time to just gaze at the piece of the whole that you are a part of.

Presenting Issue: Life is ugly. I feel ugly.

Movement: Stretch.

Affirmation: The higher I get, the better I see the whole.

Traveller's Eye

Feature # 5 of the Helpful People Endeavor

The thing that is unique to vacations is that the traveller is looking at every site with fresh eyes. He or she has not yet become accustomed to the scenery. She notices every detail which is different from her ordinary world. He is refreshed by the time and space to take a good look at what is before him.

With discipline, one can occasionally look at one's own town with the traveller's eye. Try imagining that you have never been here before. How would you describe this place to the folks back home? The traveller's eye view brings immediate clarity to the balance of beauty and ugliness which have come to reside in your landscape.

To some extent, beauty is in the eye of the beholder, but not entirely. Even if we prefer desert to ocean or pine tree forests to magnolia gardens, we as humans most always prefer a preponderance of nature to plastic and plaster. We may tolerate busy, congested streets and skyscrapers to get the artistic multi-cultural milieu of a big city, but we do not like it. We are willing to compromise.

But if compromise were not necessary, what would we prefer? We like flowers with our food, gardens with our buildings, parks with our streets, quiet places between nodes of activity. We do not mind driving, but prefer no traffic jams. In other words, we like balance. The desert would be deadly without water, the ocean frightening if we could not find land.

In order to have some of the rejuvenation happen at home which happens on vacation, we need to create the balance between opposites that truly feeds us. Pay attention to your trip to town. Are there ways you can change your route for a whole new outlook on life? With the traveller's eye, you potentially become a helpful person to yourself and to your town. Taking a new look at what you have become accustomed to can be a first step to creating a better community.

Presenting Issue: I feel out of sorts. I sense something is wrong, but I do not know what.

Movement: Close your eyes. Breathe deeply. Open them as if you are new on the scene.

Affirmation: Long may I travel, seeing life's beauty.

Correction of Misuse
Feature #6 of the Helpful People Endeavor

Each of us has our own opinions about what constitutes misuse. There are a variety of cultural, religious and social values which guide us in our choices. The important issue, however, is not to attempt to come to an empirical right or wrong, but to take responsibility for bringing your personal world up to par with your own value system.

You can clean up your own house. Clean up your own

relationship to the Earth in your own backyard, especially if you are renting or otherwise temporary, for these often become the most abused properties. You can even go beyond your own back yard and begin to claim a portion of the neighborhood which no one else ever claims. That is, take responsibility for a vacant lot, a street or a run-down building. Plant seeds, pick up trash. Paint and repair. Dwell there - in the place you have chosen - in spirit for some part of each day.

Everywhere in America, there are cities and towns with places that have lost their standing as meaningful to human beings and which can no longer serve any but the most basic forms of life due to the way human beings have left them. In other words, when the humans moved on, they left concrete shells or clear-cut woods. They did not remove their buildings nor restore nature properly so that wildlife could come again and make the place home. And they did not maintain the human constructions so that other humans could follow and be sheltered or uplifted by what they left behind.

Instead, we have junkyards of every scale. We are the reapers of incredible ignorance, and, though we might be able to say, "It is not my fault," we, nevertheless, are the only ones left to clean up the mess. We may not be able to do this with much love for the "previous tenants," but we can do it with love for Earth herself, mother of all nature, bringer of life. We can offer our work with glad hearts that she still bestows us with billions of seeds for our food plants and myriad forms of beauty.

Presenting Issue: I often complain about others. My disposition is bad.

Movement: Bend.

Affirmation: Without need to blame, I calmly reclaim Mother Earth.

Beneficial Relationship
Feature #7 of the Helpful People Endeavor

We are so used to thinking "people" when we hear the word relationship; but we are in relationship to all that is. We are in our most important and potentially beneficial relationship to Earth. A relationship is a two-way process of giving and receiving. The Earth is always making her gifts obvious, yet, as a culture, perhaps even as a world, we tend to overlook them or to think that her gifts are to be taken completely for our own personal benefit without any thought of sharing.

Earth offers trees, stones, metals, wind, sun, water and time. She is the first ingredient in all things created. Creator has given us one planet with which to shape a life of beauty, reverence and wonder. There is no current scientific evidence that another Earthlike environment awaits us anywhere in the known Universe. Our idea of paradise may be just a cellular memory of the Earth that once was or could be.

Earth is the immediate source of our life. Try to go without her food for a week to bring this lesson home. If you manage that, see how long you can go without water. You will realize your humble dependence in no time. Fortunately, Earth wants to feed and shelter you, to provide a rich, beautiful life. It is only civilization which interferes with or assists this process. Whatever you take of Earth's bounty, acknowledge her power and give thanks. She is your greatest benefactor.

Presenting Issue: I am lonely. I feel isolated. I do not feel at home here.

Movement: Lie down on the ground outdoors with as little between you and the earth as possible.

Affirmation: I am helped every step of my way.

Health

Our health and the health of the Earth are one. Nourishment comes from the living garden that grows around our lives.

The Seven Features of the Health Endeavor

1. Hint of a Spirit
2. Invitation To Enter
3. Seed of Self
4. Hidden Sanctuary
5. Nature's Intention
6. A Place To Be Poor
7. Rest At the End

Hint of a Spirit

Feature #1 of the Health Endeavor

Go look out your back door. Whatever is there, claim it. It is your given territory for now. Perhaps forever. Make it your enchanted garden. It does not matter if yesterday you thought of it as a slum. Today, it begins a new life as an enchanted garden.

You might also look at yourself, your body. It too is your territory for now, for better or worse, until death do you part. Your body really does not want to wait for paradise in the hereafter. It wants to return to the garden now. You are going to give it that chance.

Go outside. Look around for the spot which is the most interesting to you. Whenever you find a place that touches you, ask whether you might come into an apprenticeship there. If you feel the place has spirit, whether you "see" one or not, it probably does. It hardly matters whether you believe in fairies, nature spirits or can see the auras of trees, the important thing is that you allow the possibility. Have no expectations. Just return often with an attitude of reverence. Allow whatever happens.

If you feel something different, something different is there. In this place where you are attracted, make an offering. Ask how you might be of benefit. Carry out the inspiration that comes. Return with appreciation. Ask again. Act again in behalf of the place. Continue this process as often as you can, treating the place as a sacred spot.

Be open, sincere, see what happens.

Presenting Issue: The places I loved are gone. I feel I cannot return to an earlier, better time.

Movement: Walk outdoors naked (if you can) or observe your naked body in a mirror. Where is there life?

Affirmation: The Great Mystery is always in place.

Invitation To Enter
Feature #2 of the Health Endeavor

After you have discovered the most magical place, design your garden around it.   Make a gateway.   It could be an arbor, ribbons, a banner, anything to form an arch.   Trim a bush. Prop up sticks. Make a fence. Or lay some stones. Use whatever is within your means to create something that says, "Here is the way in." Do it your way. Be playful. Get excited about it. You are not merely working here; you are making a place for hidden pleasure. There is no one you need to please here except yourself.

By pleasing yourself, you will probably delight whoever may be privileged to later enter your domain. But right now, it is you and Mother Earth. You are the Grand High Priestess in this, her local temple. In this temple you are going to make amends for any defilement of the Earth which has taken place on this land. Even if you are blessed with a lovely green lawn and previously planted perennials, at one time, the soil was probably bulldozed or there may have been an ancient battle fought on this very ground. Whatever errors have been committed on this land, you are going to correct by turning it into a sacred place.

You start this process by creating the entrance. It need only be inviting to your soul, that deep, rich part of you that is one with Mother Earth. To please your soul is to please her. As you create the entrance to this secret garden, know that you are being initiated as Her High Priestess in this, the temple which she has given you. When your entrance is complete, pass through.

Realize that you are in yet another temple. Your own body. Decide to enter into it as well. Just be there, in yourself, in the garden.

Presenting Issue: I do not want to go out. I feel like hibernating.

Movement: Sit still, softly gazing at your spot of land until it moves you. Notice what moved you.

Affirmation: I am enchanted by the land outside my door.

Seed of Self
Feature #3 of the Health Endeavor

Somewhere in your garden, allow a wild place to exist, a place for nature's creatures to live without interruption by human beings. Let this be your own small wilderness. This honors the wild place in yourself and respects the integrity of the plants and animals as a self-sustaining community. They may offer you many teachings if you simply allow them to be and watch how they live together.

Once your wild place is designated, it is wise to be aware that everywhere you go, you are bringing your own consciousness with you. Your habits, desires and shortcomings will all tend to follow you and leave their affect on each place you enter. One should at least wonder what that affect might be and question whether or not it will benefit the place. In your own garden, your intentions are probably clear. But in any other wilderness area, remember, you are entering into the territory of others, and it is proper to seek permission.

There is little enough territory left for nature's wild creatures where they can live without human interruption. Whenever you are entering wild land, stop, listen, see if you can get an intuitive sense of whether you are being invited to enter. Clear your mind and let your intention be made known. Send out the thought of what you seek and what you are offering in return.

If you are welcomed or, at worst, are uncertain of your inner knowing, enter peacefully, respecting the landscape as it is. If you are attempting to form a sacred relationship with this wild place, let that be known. You may wish to offer a gift of a small pinch of corn meal or tobacco, traditional native gifts to the spirit of a place, or some other substance which is important to your life.

To form sacred relationship, you must also become a gift to the wild place yourself. Take time here to contemplate who you are and in what ways you could possibly be of benefit to the forest, field, beach, stream or backyard you are befriending. What is the seed of self you plant here? How will the animals, plants and weather of this place help you to grow and be nourished?

Away-from-home places often give us our first magical earth experience. Perhaps you have walked the Grand Canyon or sailed the Great Lakes or visited a majestic mountain where, for a moment or a day you were swept away into a numinous experience. All of a sudden, there in the wild unknown, you came to a clearing. It might have been a calmness of the waters, a widening of the trail, an inlet, a crossroads or an empty place. The landscape changed and so did you. The land, by its nature, leads the psyche to soul awareness.

Cherish these moments and these places, for without both the wilderness and the natural clearing, our souls are lost. To preserve the land is to preserve the richness of our own lives. As you practice your earthkeeping art in your own back yard, you will become ever more aware of your attitude toward all land and of other people's attitudes and actions toward the Earth. All the world will begin to seem like your own personal sanctuary, and you will want others to care for Mother Earth just as respectfully as you do. In this regard, your actions - how you treat your own home land - will be the greatest teacher.

As you become clear on how you wish to treat your personal part of Mother Earth's body, your home plot will be the clearing of the harmful attitudes shown to Her by others. You will be a clearing in the woods, a sanctuary of wild wisdom, a teaching seed for a new world.

Presenting Issue: I feel unimportant.

Movement: In a secluded spot, go wild.

Affirmation: Everywhere I go, I leave a soft and deep impression.

Hidden Sanctuary
Feature #4 of the Health Endeavor

If you are going to create your sacred relationship with a piece of land at home, begin by arranging for some privacy. If your yard itself is not private, use shrubbery, fencing, shades, cloth or anything else you have to create a private area. You are building a sanctuary for your soul, a place where the birds, butterflies and other of nature's beautiful beings will gather and heal you.

Some part of the garden is best invitingly exposed, so that you can see it from inside the house. This could be the entrance gateway, the path from your door, the tops of flowering trees, a statue, the vegetable growing part of the plot or any other area that beckons you, offering respite from your worldly cares.

Libraries, bookstores and seed catalogs all have books and pictures with thousands of inspiring ways to set up your garden. Look up headings like "Landscape Architecture," "Art," "Home Decorating," "Water Gardens," "Architecture," and "City Planning," as well as just "Gardening." You will be amazed at the infinite possibilities.

If your garden is to be a true healing sanctuary, you will want to emphasize the four elements in its creation: soil, wind, heat, and water. These are always present in some form; but it is good to accentuate them. You might make an especially rich soil mound adding compost or peat moss and honor it with a flamboyant flower. You might site a bench to catch the evening breeze and hang a wind sock or a chime to sing the wind's song. You can capture heat with a southern orientation or a reflecting wall, or make a firepit for ceremonies in the yard. Water can be the rain resting in the birdbath or a seashell; or you could construct a fountain or a pond. A harmonious blend of the elements in your hidden garden sanctuary will tend to bring about a similar balance in yourself.

Presenting Issue: I lack a sense of well-being.

Movement: Bathe outdoors.

Affirmation: In my secret garden, I am healed.

Nature's Intention

Feature #5 of the Health Endeavor

Whenever you begin working with land or just forming a friendly relationship with Earth in general, be sure to observe and listen for nature's intention. What process is she involved in here? Are your plans in harmony with hers?

Which way do the waters flow when it rains? Will you be changing this direction? Will your building or path cause erosion? Are there deer trails or feeding grounds for other wildlife you will be destroying? Where will they go instead? Will your building block the sun or the view for someone else? Take some time not only to mentally assess the pros and cons of your proposed environmental changes, but to feel. Sense the Mother there, listen to the life. What does she want? How does she feel about your plans?

In a crowded world, it is not always possible to give nature free reign. Compromises are made. Wherever your will and the will of the land are at odds and you choose to have your way, make an offering. Plant several trees for each one that must come down. The nurturing energy fields of mature trees are not duplicated by the tiny forcefield of a single seedling. Use the wood wisely that is harvested from your land. Make a prayer in the manner that comes to you.

If you build your house in the place where the earth always shifts or the water flows freely, your house will be in jeopardy. If you pay no attention to the wind and sun, you could lose the warmth and brightness that make so much difference in your daily mood. It is natural and beneficial to live in the most beautiful area you can find, but request the guidance of nature there before you claim the spot for your dwelling. You are planning to be together a long time, and she is so much stronger and wiser than you, it is best to start out friends.

Once you are friends, you will have an intuitive sense about what needs to be planted or removed and how to care for your garden. Whether you grow food, flowers or just work with the wilds, your enchanted garden will nourish your soul as long as you care for its spirit.

Presenting Issue: I often feel the world is against me.

Movement: Dance with a tree.

Affirmation: Humbly, I place myself in harmony with nature's plan.

A Place To Be Poor

Feature #6 of the Health Endeavor

In all times, there have been those who by fate or by choice are poor. There is the hermit, trying to live a simple life, close to the Earth, to discover spiritual truth or pursue a singular intent. There are the unfortunate who without luck or lacking diligence find themselves penniless. There are the homeless, the distraught and the dangerous.

For the most part, we have designated no place for any

of them. The institutionalized are such by virtue of money. The poor are yet free. All of these many varieties of people are guests, people passing through who need meals and lodging. They are our guests until we find a place for them in society, a use and a value to their existence. They depend upon us. We hope a handout will see them on their way, but we have no place for them.

Would it not be better, here and there, scattered throughout the country, cities and nation, to set aside land for squatters? Let a group of poor homestead lots on a city block? Claim a half acre of land needing care? Give the right to just be there, without needing to work, to build or to do anything whatsoever. Give the right to make do, to scavenge and create a lean-to and cook over an open fire in a tin can without getting arrested, without, by default, trespassing or loitering.

Call it the right of gypsies or a place for pilgrims or just an experiment to allow the dignity of one's own choice or circumstance. A city could supply basic hygiene facilities cheaper than a welfare system, housing projects and rescue missions. Being poor is only a crime when we outlaw basic existence. Being poor could be a spiritual quest or a valid lifestyle on a healing planet. But to be anything good, being poor must have a place.

Presenting Issue: I am upset with others who seem to be unable to care for themselves. I am burdened with the complexity of life.

Movement: See if you can find a place to spend the night without shelter, camping gear or money.

Affirmation: For every person under heaven, in my world a place is given.

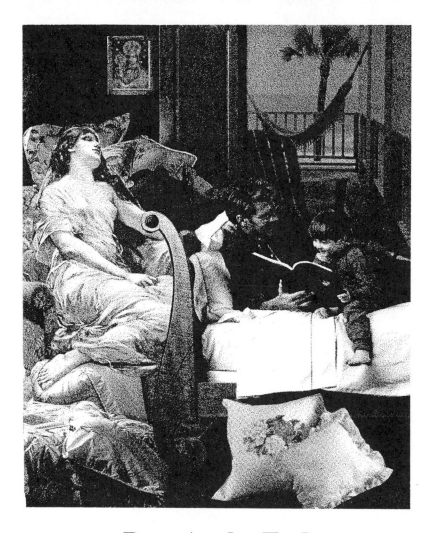

Rest At the End
Feature #7 of the Health Endeavor

Whether at the end of your day, the end of a path, or the end of your life, rest should be the reward. See to it that your journey has a place to stop. It is in this pause that review happens, breath is taken, and life continues.

Give yourself and your guests a bench, some refreshment, a view of past or possibility. Let there be a sign that designates that this is the culmination. Here you can

contemplate the Great Mystery, doze or dream. here, after all your turns and trials is the boundary of this experience.

It may be a day that has passed, a season, a phase of life or a lifetime. We are older now, wiser by our experience. After our rest, we shall begin again. All that we have left behind can nurture others. If we have lived with reverence for the Earth, she will live on in eternal fertility to nourish generations to come. We can give thanks for the wondrous adventure she took us on and say good-bye with the setting sun. A new day will come and it will be the richer for our having lived. May it be a glorious day. May there be rest for all at the end.

Presenting Issue: I fear death. I cannot let go. I lack trust in Creation.

Movement: Sleep.

Affirmation: All things die. All things begin again.

Index

Recommended Reading

Sacred Space & Wild Grace
Interior Design with Feng Shui, Sarah Rossbach, E. P. Dutton, 1987.
Living Color, Master Lin Yun's Guide to Feng Shui and the Art of Color, Sarah Rossbach & Lin Yun, Kodansha International, 1994.

Career
The Medicine Woman's Guide To Being In Business For Yourself, How to Live by Your Spiritual Vision in a Money-based World, Carol Bridges, Earth Nation, 1992.

Self-Knowledge
Care of the Soul, A Guide for Cultivating Depth and Sacredness in Everyday Life, Thomas Moore, Walker & Co., 1993.
The Medicine Woman Tarot, Carol Bridges, U.S. Games Systems, Inc., 1990.
The Medicine Woman Inner Guidebook, A Woman's Guide to Her Unique Powers, Carol Bridges, U.S. Games Systems, Inc., 1991.

Ancestors/History
How Buildings Learn, What Happens After They're Built, Stewart Brand, Viking Penguin, 1994.
The Sacred, Ways of Knowledge, Sources of Life, Peggy V. Beck & A. L. Walters, Navajo Community College Press, 1977.

Wealth
Your Money or Your Life, Transforming Your Relationship with Money and Achieving Financial Independence, Joe Dominguez & Vicki Robin, Penguin Books, 1993.

Children/Creativity
The Art of Ritual, A Guide to Performing Your Own Rituals for Growth and Change, Renee Beck & Sydney Barbara Metrick, Celestial Arts, 1990.
Keepers of the Earth, Native American Stories and Environmental Activities for Children, Michael J. Caduto & Joseph Bruchac, Fulcrum, Inc., 1989.
No More Second Hand Art, Awakening the Artist Within, Peter London, Shambhala, 1987.

Helpful People/Community
Ceremonial Circle, Practice, Ritual and Renewal for Personal and Community Healing, Sedonia Cahill & Joshua Halpern, Harper San Francisco, 1992.
A Pattern Language, Towns, Buildings, Construction, Christopher Alexander, Sara Ishikawa & Murray Silverstein, Oxford University Press, 1977.

Health/Earth
The Earth Manual, How to Work On Wild Land Without Taming It, Malcolm Margolin, Heydey Books, 1985.
Earth Ponds, the Country Pond-maker's Guide to Building, Maintenance and Restoration, Tim Matson, Countryman Press, 1991.
Healing Environments, Your Guide to Indoor Well-Being, Carol Venolia, Celestial Arts, 1988.
Places of the Soul, Christopher Day, Aquarian Press, 1990.
Sacred Land, Sacred Sex, Rapture of the Deep, Concerning Deep Ecology and Celebrating Life, Dolores LaChapelle, Kwaki Press, 1988.

Lectures/Workshops/Training
Sacred Place Practitioner Training, a year-long course of home study and workshops with Carol Bridges. Contact Earth Nation, PO Box 743, Nashville, IN 47448, 812-988-0873
Yun Lin Temple, 2959 Russell St., Berkeley, CA 94705, 510-841-2347, sponsors Master Li Yun's feng shui lectures throughout the world.